WAR
AND
SPACE

ROBERT SALKELD

Foreword by General B. A. Schriever
U.S. Air Force, Retired.

PRENTICE-HALL, INC.
Englewood Cliffs, N.J.

In memory of my grandfather,
Henry F. Salkeld,
who first told me about space

FOREWORD

The pace of scientific discovery and of technological progress continues to accelerate. It is accelerating so rapidly that it represents a special form of threat to this country and its democratic form of government.

Our system of government demands that the people be informed in order for them to make sound judgments about national issues. Our system also provides a means through popular elections of insuring that our governmental programs are created and administered by the most knowledgeable and the most competent citizens.

Today, the average citizen, intelligent and educated though he may be, is finding it extremely difficult to maintain even a basic understanding of the latest scientific and technological developments. And government officials often write laws and administer programs without fully appreciating the applications of technology to the problems they are attempting to solve.

In short, there is a lag between scientific discovery and its translation into national policy. And that lag is growing greater.

Since World War II, the public has increasingly lost touch with the implications of the scientific and technological revolution on the status of national security. And the public has failed to stay informed—largely because information has not been made available—about the manner in which the Soviet Union has been vigorously pursuing all areas of technology and then rapidly applying all advances to enhancing their military posture.

In past years, our national leaders and the members of the press gave to the public the basic facts about nuclear weapons and ballistic missiles. They also explained that the only logical military policy for a non-aggressive nation, such as ours, in a nuclear age was one of deterrence. They stressed that the only way to keep an aggressive nation from using its nuclear power to destroy or to intimidate us was for us to be able to retaliate (from an initial blow) with sufficient power to insure the destruction of the aggressor's social and economic structure.

Today our strategic deterrence appears in jeopardy because the Soviets have developed strategic weapons which threaten the survivability of our retaliatory force. In 1969 the Secretary of Defense several times testified to Congress that the Soviet SS-9 ICBM with multiple warheads is a first-strike system. Also in light of the tremendous Soviet naval buildup it is dangerous to assume that our ballistic missile submarine force will remain invulnerable. Finally there is clear evidence that strategic superiority has passed to the Soviets or is now in the process of doing so.

The deterioration of the U.S. strategic posture has led many to conclude that our only recourse is strategic arms limitation agreements with the Soviet Union. It is, of course, the sincere hope of every logical person that an agreement can be reached with the Soviet Union for strategic arms control. However, an honest interpretation of Communist doctrine and of Soviet history does not suggest that we should place high hopes that an accord can be reached which will guarantee our security. There-

iv

fore, it is essential that we vigorously search for other strategic capabilities to provide additional options.

Is there an alternative to disarmament negotiations if they should fail? Robert Salkeld says the answer is "Yes." I agree.

That answer lies in the most advanced field of technology, namely space technology. It lies in the development of strategic space weapons.

Robert Salkeld describes these weapons and the manner in which they could re-establish the credibility of our strategic deterrence. Although Mr. Salkeld is a prominent scientist, he has written about war and space in clear descriptive terms and with a logic that compels attention. His book is for the general public, especially that portion of the public which wishes to remain informed.

There will be those who will contend—more loudly than clearly—that Mr. Salkeld is simply advocating another round in the arms race, or posing another provocation to the Soviet Union. In fact, he is doing neither. He is facing the facts of Soviet diplomatic history and the facts of recent Soviet strategic arms developments, and he is offering to this country a way in which we may apply technology to provide for our national security, if this is necessary. It is a way which has so far been overlooked or ignored.

Mr. Salkeld is not advocating that we do something simply because it is technically feasible. He is not arguing that space weapons are best simply because they are exotic. He is saying that if the Soviet Union continues to build strategic weapons which threaten our ability to retaliate, then we can and should proceed to re-establish our strategic posture through strategic space weapons.

In my judgment, responsible citizens and government officials should understand the kinds of strategic space weapons that can be built—by the Soviet Union as well as by the United States. And they should also understand the concept of deterrence which these weapons could provide.

We have sacrificed the strategic superiority we once enjoyed in order to produce an atmosphere, a rapport, which would be conducive to negotiations. It would be a tragedy of historic proportions for this country to negotiate with the Soviet Union on strategic arms limitations on the assumption that there was no way, technically, to re-establish our strategic deterrence.

Lack of information and lack of public understanding have always been enemies of democracy. But never have they posed more of a threat than they do today. In *War and Space*, Mr. Salkeld has made a major contribution to this country by supplying some urgently needed information which deserves the conscientious attention of every citizen and every policy maker.

General B.A. Schriever
U.S. Air Force, Retired.

PREFACE

In these early years of the space age, we are crossing the threshold to what may be man's greatest adventure. Our explorations and exploits beyond the earth could do more in the next few decades to transform our perspectives and the course of our history, than all the new horizons we ever crossed during the centuries it took us to open up the western hemisphere of our planet.

Premonitions of this momentous venture—space exploration—stretch back to the ancients. Forecasts of it began to take specific form within the last hundred years in the prophetic literature of Jules Verne and H. G. Wells, the theoretical writings of Konstantin Tsiolkovsky and Hermann Oberth, and the technical and experimental work of Robert Goddard. In the early twentieth century a new literary form, called science fiction, gained favor and won a large and avid audience. Since the space age actually arrived with the launching of Sputnik 1, books and articles of a more factual nature attempting to explore the implications of space for all imaginable human activities, have literally poured forth.

We are deluged with serious speculation about what can, should and will be accomplished in space, from scientific data gathering, global satellite communications, weather and resource mapping and the improvement of industrial processes, to the mining and colonization of the moon and planets, travel to the stars and the search for extraterrestrial life. Not even such possibilities as orbital resort hotels and vacations on the moon have been overlooked.

The reader would therefore be justified in asking my reasons for adding yet another book to this growing mountain of speculation. My answer is simple. There is a key element of the space age which, improbable as it may seem, has received virtually no open and serious attention at all: the political and military implications of space as an arena for strategic systems and operations. Its neglect has resulted in part from the difficulty of trying to imagine and pin down at a practical level, the implications of an arena so new, vast and strange compared with the familiar land, sea and air theaters of the earth. It has also resulted from government policies which have strained to divert public attention toward the peaceful uses of space and away from its military aspects.

Yet it is more evident each year that the strategic implications of space may have a profound bearing on the future not only of international affairs in general, but of the arms race in particular, our own way of life, and even our very survival. As more advanced space capabilities are developed by the United States, the Soviet Union and inevitably other powers as well, a failure to face these questions directly could allow us to drift into great danger.

Inevitably the issue must be opened up for discussion, and that is the purpose of this book. It will question the wishful slogan, "Space is for peace," and the comfortable idea that space is an esoteric subject that can be treated apart from our affairs here on earth. It will contest the familiar notion that aside from certain supporting activities such as reconnaissance, communications, navigation and meteorology, space offers little of military value. It will argue that space is in fact an arena of unprecedented strategic potential, and that it may offer one of the few realistic resolutions to the ever more threatening and puzzling dilemma of the arms race.

Given the perspective of history, the slowness and difficulty with which the strategic and political implications of space are coming to be understood and appreciated are not surprising.

In the classic example of the oceans, nearly four hundred years would pass—empires would rise and fall—after they were opened up by the fifteenth century voyages of exploration, before the roles of ocean commerce and naval power in shaping the course of history, were expressed in a systematic way by Alfred Mahan in 1890. Once articulated, this understanding of the meaning of the seas and seapower, has been credited with influencing directly the policies of President Theodore Roosevelt and Kaiser Wilhelm II. In a broader sense the very patterns of both world wars, and the emergence of the United States as a world power are traceable to Mahan's theories.

Over shorter time periods, the economic and strategic implications of the atmospheric and undersea environments have been identified and appreciated only after periods of confusion, controversy and on occasion bitter struggle. Allied indecision about the military importance of airpower, submarines and ballistic missiles, contributed respectively, to the success of the German blitzkriegs of 1939 and 1940, to near-disaster in the Battle of the North Atlantic in 1941, and to a Soviet head start in ballistic missile and space technology in the 1950's, which was overcome only through an extraordinary crash program of research and development.

Now confusion abounds with regard to space, as in

the previous opening of new arenas. Some enthusiasts visualize far flung systems of space stations, extraterrestrial bases and fleets of spacecraft performing a broad variety of scientific, commercial and military functions, while those less enchanted see only an insatiable money sink swallowing up funds for exotic activities, unrelated to what they consider more pressing social and economic needs.

The very question of military space activities might appear to have been settled by the Space Treaty of 1967. Yet this treaty, which prohibits the "stationing" of "weapons of mass destruction" in "outer space," does not define any of those terms, provide for inspection of launch sites or orbiting devices, nor does it include any provision for enforcement. Further, the subsequent development and deployment of a fractional orbital bombardment system (FOBS) by the Soviet Union, and defense of their right to do so under the Space Treaty by United States officials, surely indicates an uncertain future for that treaty as a viable instrument.

Appreciation of the contributions of space activities to national security has been inhibited by a United States policy of secrecy regarding almost all information about Department of Defense satellite operations, which has been rigidly in effect since April, 1962. Yet the press persistently report that of the hundreds of satellites launched to date by the United States and the Soviet Union, nearly half have been for strategic surveillance. While such activity does not violate the Space Treaty, it certainly raises the likelihood of eventual military confrontation in space, if the U-2, *Pueblo* and other such incidents are to be interpreted as providing any kind of precedents.

The experience of history therefore suggests that it would be unwise for the subject of military implications of space to long remain veiled. The course of events gives increasingly clear evidence that it cannot remain so in view of presently developing trends in strategic weaponry.

Except in specific instances where subsequent updating has been possible, the historical accounts of arms control efforts, advancing strategic technology and the cold war in space, have been carried just through the end of the Johnson administration. Since then, the tempo of events has quickened, with dramatic demonstrations of new space capabilities in the American Apollo lunar program and the Soviet Soyuz space station project, and there have been insistent reports that a Soviet launch vehicle of unprecedented size is approaching its first flight. At the same time, disturbing intelligence has been made public by Secretary of Defense Melvin Laird, which indicates that the Soviets have been deploying their new SS-9 heavy missile in far greater numbers than previously expected. This vehicle is capable of launching multiple warheads which could be used to destroy our land-based strategic missiles in a first strike. It also serves as the booster for the Soviet fractional orbital bombardment system, which could be used as a surprise attack component against our strategic bomber and other installations. The Secretary stated that not only bomber forces and land-based missiles, but missile-launching submarines as well, may have lost much of their survivability in the event of nuclear war, as early as 1972. These facts could indicate, as he noted, that the Soviets may indeed be working to achieve a first strike capability against the United States.

Some have charged that the Secretary's statements may have been overdrawn in an effort to support the Safeguard ABM system proposed by President Nixon. Yet such testimony from a Secretary of Defense cannot but increase the seriousness of our concern about the diminishing survivability of our strategic systems and the resulting increase in the precariousness of the "balance of terror."

It is to be hoped that at long last, diplomatic efforts toward arms control and disarmament can somehow find a solid basis of agreement for at least strengthening that balance, and perhaps even defusing the arms race, as a result of the Strategic Arms Limitation Talks (SALT) between the United States and the Soviet Union. The long history of similar efforts, however, affords us scant grounds to count on such a triumph. These talks must be pursued with abiding determination and good faith, but experience and common sense require us to search at the same time for other ways to stabilize the deterrent balance, in the event that we cannot achieve in practice the necessary levels of international trust and cooperation, through diplomacy alone.

This book is part of that search, and it is my hope that it will encourage fresh thinking about a few of the critical questions of war, space, and the future.

Robert Salkeld

CONTENTS

CONTENTS

INTRODUCTION

In the two centuries since the Industrial Revolution, the destructiveness of man's armaments has so expanded that in any future large-scale war devastation could not be confined to the battlefields and oceans but would spill across the entire planet. It is doubtful whether civilization could survive such an onslaught without regressing hundreds or thousands of years.

The response to this mounting threat has been more than 150 years of nearly continuous efforts to stop war and call a halt to the spiraling arms race. This long quest included an arms reduction proposal as early as 1816 by Czar Alexander I in the wake of the Napoleonic wars. After that, increasingly insistent arms control efforts were initiated after each of the major conflicts for the next century: the Crimean, the American Civil, the Franco-Prussian and the Russo-Japanese War. In the aftermath of the First World War, disarmament activities became a permanent function in the League of Nations and, following the Second World War, in the United Nations. Since World War II, these activities have centered around the Geneva Disarmament Conferences and negotiations leading to the Antarctic Treaty of 1959, the Limited Nuclear Test Ban Treaty of 1963, the Space Treaty of 1967 and the Nuclear Nonproliferation Treaty of 1970.

What has been achieved? The hard fact is that despite

the degree of honest and sincere concern behind these efforts, men have apparently been unable to control either the development or proliferation of increasingly destructive armaments by diplomatic means. Fortunately we seem to have been able to reach peaceful solutions to a great many problems over the years. In certain instances those solutions may have resulted partly from the relief of tensions afforded by diplomatic agreements. But there are strong reasons to think that such solutions have generally and more fundamentally depended on balances of power based on strategic military capabilities, which no major state has been [or appears to be] willing to relinquish, or suffer to be limited.

On a steady diet of accelerating technology, strategic armaments have outgrown their traditional arena, the earth. Yet neither history nor the current facts of life give any real hope that in the foreseeable future the arms race can be controlled or that war can be effectively outlawed. And, as world populations continue to grow and the economic gulf widens between the wealthy few and the poor multitudes, the probability of increasingly bitter and widespread warfare can only mount.

The obvious basic solutions to this dilemma, which almost anyone can recite with very little thought, are population and arms control, and improved education and standards of living. The problem with these kinds of remedies is that even if some of them are achievable on the practical level, which is certainly open to question, they are long-term processes and their beneficial effects could not be felt for several decades. They cannot solve the more immediate problem of survival in the next twenty- or thirty-year period, which threatens to be a time of rising discontent and proliferating nuclear and bio-chemical weapons.

What, then, are the alternatives? There appear to be only two:

The first alternative is to let the survival of civilized societies depend entirely on our ability to avoid general war by means of the currently existing system of strategic deterrence until pursuit of some of the above longer-term goals yields results. But deterrence depends primarily on the ability of strategic systems to survive attack, with strength sufficient to retaliate so heavily that the would-be attacker is unwilling to risk striking in the first place. Such survivability has been assured in the past by protecting strategic weapons in fixed underground silos and in mobile carriers such as bombers and submarines. This survivability, however, is constantly being eroded by advances in the technologies of reconnaissance, antiaircraft systems, antisubmarine warfare, missile guidance accuracy and multiple warheads. Inevitably, and perhaps sooner than generally believed, no earthbound weapon system will be adequately secure from detection, surveillance and massive on-target attack. The dependability of deterrent systems on earth, then, is melting away and with it the credibility of the strategic balance on which we have relied to deter nuclear war.

The second alternative is to maintain our earthbound deterrent as long as possible by improving the effectiveness of our submarines and the striking power of our missiles, and trying to defend them with other missiles; meanwhile developing the technologies necessary to gain the enhanced survivability which in the long run can be preserved only in deep space. Even in the vicinity of the earth where terrestrial gravity prevails and orbits around the earth can be sustained, our entire planet occupies less than one millionth the total volume of these regions. It is a mere speck of dust. Because of the awesome size of the new arena of space, deployment of strategic systems in deep space promises unprecedented degrees of survivability, mainly because they would be insulated by astronomically large distances and thus able essentially to hide in vast, still unexplored regions.

Beyond merely enhancing survivability it seems quite possible that the addition of the space dimension to strategic warfare could introduce a further deterrent factor. Certainly it would cause a would-be attacker to reevaluate the feasibility and probable consequences of such an action. And it appears reasonable to expect that because of the vastness of the space arena any strategic competition there would develop, at worst, into a kind of cold war of attrition—in which sporadic hostile actions could be confined to space and not rebound to earth.

Increased ability to hide and operate covertly would, on the other hand, be a tempting objective for a potential aggressor, for it would enhance his capability to launch surprise attacks. Thus, there appear to be natural reasons why *both* deterrent and potentially aggressive powers would be motivated to extend their strategic capabilities to deep space. As a result, the second alternative may ultimately be the inevitable one.

The Space Treaty, however, stands squarely in the path of the extension of strategic capabilities to space. Article IV of the treaty provides:

> States party to the Treaty undertake not to place in orbit around the Earth any objects carrying nuclear weapons or any other kinds of weapons of mass destruction, install such weapons on celestial bodies, or station such weapons in outer space in any other manner.

The treaty further forbids the establishment of military bases, installations, fortifications, the testing of weapons and the conducting of military maneuvers on celestial bodies. It requires that all stations, installations, equipment and space vehicles on celestial bodies be open to inspection by other states on a reciprocal basis, given reasonable advance notice. It is silent with regard to inspection of launch operations and orbiting objects, and contains no provision for enforcement.

This confronts us with a very threatening situation. If strategic armaments are confined to the earth, as the Space Treaty intends, then our survival hangs wholly on our ability to avoid large-scale war—by either formal or tacit agreement, *essentially forever*. Yet all our attempts to avoid general war have failed not once, but several times in modern history. Therefore, should we risk our very existence on the hope of accomplishing something in which we have so consistently been unsuccessful? And, may it not be that the Space Treaty, however well-intended, attempts to do exactly the wrong thing? Perhaps, but this may be academic anyway, since the developing realities of the Cold War already appear to be overtaking the Space Treaty, even as events have overtaken so many of its predecessor agreements in the past.

Actually, the Space Treaty was primarily the result of unilateral initiatives by the United States government, which has followed a policy of stressing the peaceful uses of space, while de-emphasizing space's strategic implications by means of a security clampdown on its military satellite programs; and official, though not very convincing, denials of the military value of weapons in orbit. Despite America's painstaking efforts to stamp a peaceful expression on our space program, and despite the Soviet's signature on and lip service to the treaty, they have nonetheless pushed ahead with a determined drive to develop orbital weapons capability. First their drive produced Scrag, an orbital missile unveiled in 1965. Then on November 3, 1967, just 24 days after the Space Treaty went into effect, Secretary of Defense McNamara announced that the Soviets had developed a fractional orbital bombardment System (FOBS). FOBS can orbit nuclear bombs so they can approach their targets from several directions, then be de-orbited and brought down on earth targets with only three minutes' warning. Initially, FOBS is a serious threat to cities and "soft" military targets such as warning systems, strategic bombers and their bases. With improved accuracies and larger or multiple warheads, however, FOBS could grow to be a surprise attack threat to such "hardened" military targets as strategic missiles in their concrete silos, and mobile targets such as missile-launching submarines.

Recently, official hints of the increasing vulnerability of our Polaris/Poseidon missile submarine force have begun to surface as in the following dialogue from hearings before the Senate Armed Services Committee on March 20, 1969:

> Senator Symington: Is there any reason to believe that our Poseidon force will be vulnerable to preemptive attack during the early 1970's?
>
> Secretary of Defense Laird: If this particular question is limited to the period through 1972–73, I would say I believe that our force will remain very free from attack. If you go beyond that time period, I would have to question that seriously, and I would be very happy in our executive sessions to get into the pos-

sibilities of some of the new things that are taking place in this area.

As missile-carrying submarines and surface ships become more detectable and subject to attack, their usefulness will fade very rapidly because they are inherently such attractive targets. The Poseidon submarine, for example, carries sixteen missiles (48 independent warheads if each missile carries three warheads), and all of this costly striking force as well as the sub itself, could be destroyed by a single attacking warhead—a very unfavorable exchange ratio, to say the least.

Government officials and other apologists in the United States, have made reassuring public statements that FOBS is not a violation of the Space Treaty. Using the curious rationalization that an object in orbit is not really in orbit unless it completes at least one full circuit of the earth, they claim that FOBS, therefore, is only analogous to a ballistic missile except that it uses a different kind of trajectory. As will be pointed out later, these arguments are not convincing, and use of them by the United States to defend the legitimacy of FOBS within the letter and spirit of the Space Treaty, indicates a clouded future for the treaty as an effective instrument. Further, since the treaty makes no provisions for enforcement or launch site inspection, it seems probable that as the frequency of manned space flights increases, both the United States and the Soviet Union will grow uneasy about what the other is doing out there. Under these conditions, it must be expected that each power will quietly investigate and develop strategic capabilities on its own as protection against technological surprise by the other.

It may therefore be inevitable that maintenance of deterrent stability between the United States and the Soviet Union will result in the gradual extension of strategic systems and operations into the space arena, the treaty notwithstanding.

The Soviet Union appears to be moving in this direction with FOBS. Such a process could lead to deep-space systems promising sufficient military advantages to both sides, so that a progressive reduction of earthbound strategic systems and weapon stockpiles might eventually result. Although it seems unlikely that the extension of strategic capability to space could ever eliminate city and population targeting, yet, could it not be expected in the event of a nuclear exchange that the megatonnage exploded in the atmosphere, the consequent world fallout, as well as the collateral damage to populations from attacks on nearby bomber, missile and submarine bases might be curtailed.

Such an objective is surely worthwhile. The technologies required to achieve it are already within grasp (in the sense that all required launches would be within the capability of Saturn V-class boosters and their Soviet counterparts, and that research and flight tests indicate good prospects for achieving the necessary reliability, guidance accuracies and manned stay times in space). Several unmanned spacecraft already have been guided to within a few miles of their targets on the moon, a quarter of a million miles away, and the Soviets have demonstrated comparable accuracy with their Venera 4, 5 and 6 landings on Venus. The costs, while high, appear within reason in view of the fact that in the post-1975 era when such systems could be anticipated, the Gross National Product

(GNP) of the United States is expected to exceed, and that of the Soviet Union to approach, the trillion dollar level.

A major national commitment would be required soon if the key capabilities essential for strategic space systems are to be available as the need for them develops. A new U.S. space commitment is needed in any case, since support has lagged, direction is lacking, and both civilian and military U.S. programs are floundering. This appears to have resulted mainly from fears that development of strategic space systems would give rise to an unwarranted escalation of the arms race, and from the immediate responses both the war in Vietnam and domestic urban problems necessitate. However, a more fundamental factor is the characteristic American distrust of bureaucratic concentrations of power.

The scope and complexity of developing and operating strategic space systems would demand centralized management structures of great size and influence, and herein lies a serious challenge to traditional American fears of power in large professional establishments, particularly the military. Even a military man like the late General Eisenhower was concerned about the potential threat of such interests. As President, while acknowledging the military potential of space, he was careful to place as much of the national space activity as possible under civilian control, by the National Aeronautics and Space Act of 1958. The warning he sounded in his 1961 farewell address has become classic:

> In the councils of government, we must guard against the acquisition of unwarranted influence,

whether sought or unsought, by the military-industrial complex. The potential for the disastrous rise of misplaced power exists and will persist.

Probably as a result of our apprehensions about placing such immense power in the hands of a few, the mere technological groundwork for military space capability has been allowed to proceed only reluctantly in the United States. The hard course of events may not permit skirting these issues much longer. National security, even survival itself may force them to be met directly, a task which could pose one of the most formidable challenges the United States will ever face.

I

A SHRINKING WORLD
IN PERIL

*Weapons change, but man who
uses them changes not at all.*
GEORGE S. PATTON

I

The fear of thermonuclear catastrophe has become so familiar that it has lost much of its edge in the quarter century since Hiroshima. For most people, conscious worry about it accomplishes little, and living with it dulls its impact. So it seems to have gradually subsided to an ever-present underlying influence, which conditions our attitudes toward life and the world in subtle but pervasive ways.

Some people apparently react by simply turning away, refusing to "think about the unthinkable." Others apparently accept it, but with scant hope of practical solutions, and go about their affairs living for the moment, not really bothering to prepare for, or think about, a future which may not be. Encouragingly, many people do hold hopes for the future, but most seem to have become accustomed to the unquestioning acceptance of assertions that the only paths to survival are avoiding large-scale wars, achieving arms control and disarmament, stemming the spread of nuclear weapons, and controlling population.

After a generation of living with the specter of nuclear and biological mass destruction, many people apparently have convinced themselves that these are the only possible solutions and that if efforts to bring them about are unsuccessful, civilization must eventually perish. Thus, the main emphasis in the quest for long term security and survival has been oriented toward escaping from the present "balance of terror" system, focusing on hopes of eliminating general wars by arms and population control.

The time is past due when more people should be asking themselves the hard questions: "In the light of everyday common sense, and in view of the results of our already long and determined efforts, to what degree

3

are these really practical goals, and to what extent should we pin our hopes on them?"

It is an inescapable fact that very little of substance has been accomplished which would permit us to hold realistic hopes of forever avoiding general war, and of achieving in the foreseeable future, disarmament or arms and population control around the globe. Indeed, there are compelling reasons to question whether any of these goals can ever be approached closely, and whether habitual preoccupation with them to the exclusion of other possibilities is not akin to chasing rainbows.

These are not pleasant considerations. In the pursuit of the desirable, it is human nature to sweep under the rug the unpleasant and troublesome. But facts are stubborn things, which eventually overtake those who would ignore them. Therefore, this discussion of war and space will begin with a straight look at the armaments race and the threat of war on earth, as a way of emphasizing that there are strong reasons to doubt the realism of attempts to replace the established order of strategic balance.

Rather than trying to escape from this system of increasingly precarious balances of power, there are good grounds for thinking that the most realistic course may in fact be to maintain that system, and to search for ways of restoring its stability through strengthened deterrence. Here is where strategic space systems could come into the picture, but further exploration of that possibility is left until later.

THE DAWNING AGE OF
PLANETARY WEAPONS

Throughout most of history, until the Industrial Revolution at the end of the eighteenth century, wars could be and most often were fought at safe distances from towns and cities. Since the beginning of the nineteenth century, however, technological advances in weapon destructiveness, delivery systems and mass production have so increased the scale and mobility of warfare that its direct effects can no longer be prevented from spilling across civilian population centers.

Early products of the Industrial Revolution which began to expand the scope and destructiveness of warfare were first, the railroads, which made possible the transportation and logistic supply of large armies over long distances, on a truly massive basis. The railroads were followed by the mass-produced repeating rifle, which resulted in an unprecedented growth and proliferation of firepower. Next came the telegraph and telephone, which made possible instant communications and control over the operations of widely dispersed military forces. And all during this period there were steady improvements in mass-produced field guns, leading to the first appearance of modern mobile heavy artillery in the form of the Krupp cannon, often credited as a key influence underlying the courses of the Franco-Prussian and First World wars. Subsequent developments, which did not reach fruition until late in the nineteenth century but which were to affect profoundly the character of warfare in the twentieth, were the Gatling rapid-fire gun, the submarine, the steamship, high explosives and the wireless.

The nineteenth century saw a succession of conflicts, which as a result of these developments were increasingly destructive, from the Napoleonic through the Crimean, American Civil, and Franco-Prussian Wars. Even then, the destruction of cities had become possible under certain circumstances, in the burning of Moscow, the siege of Sevastopol and Sherman's March to the Sea. By the mid-

5

dle of the twentieth century, with the mastering of high explosive and incendiary weapons, and tank, naval and aerial warfare techniques that had led to true land-sea-air mobility, two world wars had left scars of devastation across major continents. In these wars several great cities had been reduced to ruins, and nearly a hundred million people had perished.

Soon thereafter, the perfection of thermonuclear weapons, rocket delivery systems and chemical-biological warfare techniques firmly established man's war-making capabilities on a global scale. No one on earth could expect to be spared the effects of a war involving numbers of such weapons as, for example, the 20-megaton* thermonuclear warheads reported to be mounted on the Soviet SS-9 intercontinental missiles, code-named Scarp by NATO. Each warhead could gouge a mile-wide crater, level most structures for ten miles in all directions, start fires thirty miles away, and produce a blast cloud which could lay a lethal blanket of radioactive fallout up to 200 miles downwind within the first day. The destructive potential of biological weapons is in its own way equally impressive, although subject to considerable uncertainties resulting from unpredictable changes not only in winds, but temperatures and other weather conditions.

Thermonuclear bursts in space, where there is no atmosphere to absorb nuclear radiations, can produce their effects at even greater distances. For example, the above 20-megaton warhead could kill any astronauts in unshielded spacecraft within a sphere nearly 600 miles in diameter. This lethal zone could be reduced in size by proper spacecraft shielding, but significant reductions would require very large shielding weight penalties.

The above effects result from gamma and neutron

*Equivalent in destructive power to 20 million tons of TNT.

6

radiations. In addition, nuclear bursts also produce intense deluges of X-rays which are quickly absorbed in the atmosphere, but which can cause severe heat damage at great distances to many materials and structures in space where there is no atmospheric buffering. This phenomenon is utilized in the warheads of antimissile missiles such as the Spartan and Sprint vehicles of the U.S. Safeguard system, now being developed as a defense against accidental or unsophisticated missile attacks which such nations as Communist China might someday be tempted to make. In this system, X-radiations from the Spartan or Sprint warhead bursts would be counted upon to destroy or negate attacking warheads at great distances.

It is considered possible to build even larger thermonuclear warheads, with destructive capacities up to and beyond 1000 megatons, equivalent to one thousand millions tons of TNT. Such a device, if burst in the upper regions of the atmosphere, would heat up large masses of air, which in turn would bathe the earth below in intense heat radiation, igniting fires in combustible materials on the ground within a 400-mile-diameter circle. It appears, in fact, that there is no technical upper limit to the size of thermonuclear weapons, and it has been suggested that a bomb or system of bombs of such vast size could be assembled that it could destroy the entire planet, requiring no delivery system at all. This is usually referred to as a "doomsday machine," and however absurd the idea may seem, its strategic and political implications have been pondered seriously.

In addition to the effects described above, thermonuclear weapons of the size already stockpiled can produce floods of electrons which would so alter the electrical characteristics of the upper atmosphere that earthbound radio communications over large parts of the world would be blacked out for hours at a time. Also, the electrons emanating from the earth are captured by the earth's magnetic field in the Van Allen radiation belt girdling the planet, gradually dispersing through the entire volume of the belt. This can increase belt radiation intensities to levels which render access to near orbit space, by humans and certain kinds of instruments, practically impossible for months or years. Finally, weapon effects of such diversity and scale can be expected to produce significant alternations in weather, the character and extent of which are as yet unpredictable.

These dramatic developments in weaponry have been paralleled by equally remarkable advances in delivery systems. Along with the mastery of high explosive, chemical, biological and nuclear weapon technologies, the first half of the twentieth century also saw the achievement of: 1) improved land mobility in the form of mechanized and tank warfare; 2) expanded sea mobility in the form of navies to transport large masses of troops and equipment anywhere in the world within weeks, and submarine fleets which ranged the world exacting heavy tolls of shipping along strategic supply routes, and 3) true air mobility in the form of intercontinental bombers and global transport aircraft capable of carrying troops and equipment anywhere in the world within hours.

Since then, land-sea-air mobility has been further enhanced, particularly by the development of nuclear ships and submarines, and global jet transport and supersonic aircraft. More dramatically, the space arena has been opened by the advent of the modern rocket, which has made possible the delivery of conventional or nuclear and biological weapons to any point on the planet within minutes, by ballistic and orbital missiles. Recent development of multiple independently-targetable reentry vehicles (MIRV) even permits a single missile to hurl warheads accurately at several widely scattered targets. Against massive attacks of this order the defense of cities or military installations—even with such advanced anti-ballistic missile systems as Safeguard—approaches technical and economic hopelessness. Orbital flight has also opened up important possibilities for continuous global recon-naissance and surveillance of many critical activities such as military and industrial operations, and ship and sub-marine movements at sea.

The last few decades have thus witnessed an expan-sion in armaments technology such that the destructive-ness and reach of strategic systems have become truly planetary in scale. Weapon destructive capacity per pound has been increased two or three million times by the advent of thermonuclear warheads, and delivery systems velocities and weights have grown by a factor of a thou-sand or more in the cases of strategic rockets and giant aircraft.

Yet these developments have by no means reached an ultimate level, nor can such onrushing advances be expected to cease. Weapon destructiveness may be in-creased several thousand times further, if total annihila-tion of matter can be approached in nuclear explosions. Delivery system speeds and sizes will continue to increase, and it is not unrealistic to expect that such advances could open up the entire solar system as a strategic arena by early in the twenty-first century.

An entirely new class of weapon, the radiation beam or laser, may be materializing from current rapid progress in solid state phsysics. The development of so-called death ray weapons on a practical basis will require research to solve problems of power generation and beam focus-ing but there appear to be no basic reasons why these ob-stacles cannot be overcome in time. Radiation beam weap-ons of the type currently visualized are subject to severe atmospheric absorption, so their military usefulness within the atmosphere may be naturally limited. In space or the upper atmosphere, however, the effective ranges of such devices may be great indeed. Such weapons could thus offer an unprecedented combination of long-range, almost instantaneous delivery time and great aiming precision, which could be of revolutionary significance in the coming decades.

As a direct consequence of these onrushing advances, the time is drawing near when earthbound strategic systems can no longer be reliably secure or survivable against the global surveillance and reach, and the sudden and awesome destructiveness of planetary weapons. Submarines may remain survivable for some time after aircraft, ships and land-based missiles have become vulnerable, because of their ability to hide and move about within murky ocean volumes. But it must be regarded as inevitable as the advance of technology itself, that submarines eventually will be overtaken by satellite and various underwater detection and surveillance methods, which will place them under the constant aim of nuclear-armed missiles.

This erosion of the survivability of earthbound strategic systems seems destined to become a source of increasing apprehension in the years ahead, since it must lead to progressive lowering of the strength and stability of deterrence, and consequent escalation of the overall probabilities of war.

THE VANISHING PHANTOM
OF DISARMAMENT

The sobering picture of uncontrolled growth and proliferation of weaponry which has emerged with gathering force since the Industrial Revolution has been paralleled by an equally long history of frustrated attempts to stem this growth and proliferation by diplomatic means.

The search for practical formulas for arms control and disarmament, has been amazingly tenacious in view of the meagerness of its real accomplishments. The first formal approach to arms control in modern history seems to have been a set of arms reduction proposals in 1816 by Czar Alexander I in the aftermath of destruction by the Napoleonic Wars. Since then, practically continuous efforts have spanned more than a century and a half in thousands of conferences, which have produced countless commissions, declarations and agreements. A brief outline of this history will convey the scope and dogged exhaustiveness of past and present efforts.

In 1831, the French government proposed a program of arms reduction, which the French expanded and repeated in 1863 and 1870 after the Crimean, American Civil and Franco-Prussian Wars. These proposals led to the Brussels Conference of 1874, which issued an "International Declaration Concerning the Laws and Customs of War," prohibiting the use of poisons and gases in warfare. Interest in disarmament continued, and the last decades of the nineteenth century saw a number of private conferences and parliamentary resolutions on the subject.

The first disarmament conference of lasting import was suggested by Czar Nicholas II in a circular published in 1898, and was convened the following year at The Hague, with 26 States participating. Russia initiated the conference by proposing a freeze of five years on all land forces, and three years on naval forces, together with a ban on new guns and explosives, submarines and the discharge of projectiles or explosives from balloons. Most participants, including the United States, were extremely

11

cautious in mood, and all that was accomplished was approval of three declarations prohibiting discharge of projectiles from balloons, use of projectiles diffusing asphyxiating gases, and use of "dumdum" bullets. The United States opposed these declarations, believing that use of new weapons "might decrease the length of combat, and consequently the evils of war as well as the expenses entailed thereby." The United States accepted only the declaration on balloons, and that only on the condition it be limited to five years. The conference was successful, however, in adopting conventions for peaceful settlement of disputes, codifying laws and customs of war on land, and adapting the Red Cross Convention to naval warfare. Enough was achieved at the 1899 Hague Conference to maintain interest, and the Inter-Parliamentary Conference of 1904 asked President Theodore Roosevelt to propose a second conference. He agreed, but these efforts were smothered by the advent of the Russo-Japanese War.

After that clash, it was Russia again which took over preparations for the meeting, and the second Hague Conference was convened in 1907. With respect to disarmament, the meeting, which Germany refused to attend, resulted only in a reaffirmation that "the restriction of military charges, which are at present a heavy burden on the world, is extremely desirable for the increase of the material and moral welfare of mankind," and that "it is eminently desirable that Governments should resume the serious examination of this question." The Conference did adopt thirteen conventions on the laws of war and peaceful settlement of disputes. The 1907 Hague Conference was followed by other negotiations, particularly between England and Germany on the reduction of naval expenditures. Because of her heavy dependence on sea power England insisted on 60 percent superiority over the German fleet. These negotiations extended from 1908 to the outbreak of World War I in 1914.

In that war, all previous arms agreements were largely ignored, and both the Allies and Central Powers began to explore in practice the military potential of new weapon concepts based on the submarine, the tank, aerial reconnaissance and bombardment, and poison gas.

Following the First World War, disarmament attempts were resumed along two major lines, a continuous effort under Articles 8 and 9 of the Covenant of the League of Nations, and a series of naval conferences. (Mention should also be made of the Versailles Treaty, Article 171 of which prohibited use of gas and "analogous" weapons.) League Article 8 was based on a reference in President Woodrow Wilson's Fourteen Points, to "adequate guarantees given and taken that national armaments will be reduced to the lowest point consistent with domestic safety," and Article 9 provided for establishment of a permanent commission to advise the Council on execution of the provisions in Article 8. It is typical, however, of the history of disarmament that national interests forced wording changes in Wilson's statement even before its adoption in Article 8, which broadened it to the point of ambiguity and ineffectiveness. Japan, concerned with its own interests in the Pacific, succeeded in having "national safety" substituted for "domestic safety," and France, fearful of the potential threat of a future Germany, attached as an additional qualifying factor "the geographical situation and circumstances of each State."

From that point on, the League of Nations' efforts at disarmament were doomed. A number of commissions were formed, including the Permanent Advisory Commission for Military, Naval and Air Questions in 1920, the

Temporary Mixed Commission for the Reduction of Armaments in 1921, and the Preparatory Commission for the Disarmament Conference in 1927. The total outcome of this activity was a 1925 protocol prohibiting use of gases and bacterial weapons, ratified by 41 nations but not by the United States or Japan, and finally, the convening of the Geneva Disarmament Conference in 1932. This conference began with American proposals to abolish submarines, lethal gases, bacterial warfare and bombing from the air, and gradually bogged down to a game of political maneuvers. Conference committees continued to meet on technical questions into the late 1930's, but Germany's withdrawal from the Conference in 1933 and breach of the Versailles Treaty in 1935, spelled the end not only of League disarmament work, but of the League itself.

Meanwhile, four naval conferences had had temporary success at limiting the number of certain types of ships. The Washington Naval Conference of 1921–1922 succeeded in setting ratios of 5:5:3:3:3 for numbers of American, British, Japanese, French and Italian capital ships respectively. To deal with the problem of smaller vessels, the United States called a conference in Geneva in 1927, which met, bogged down and failed completely. The London Naval Conference of 1930 produced further accords between the United States, Britain and Japan, but no agreement between France and Italy. The second London Naval Conference in 1935, although it produced Anglo-French-American accords of minor import, essentially failed when Japan withdrew after demanding complete parity. No survey of the interbellum period would be complete without mention of the Kellogg-Briand Pact of 1928 which, in a burst of utopian optimism, provided for the renunciation of war itself. This pact, also called

14

the Declaration of Paris, was suggested by France and eventually ratified by 62 nations including the United States. All these efforts passed into history at the outbreak of World War II in 1939.

In the Second World War, as in the first, all preceding arms agreements essentially were ignored, and the world witnessed not only unlimited employment of whatever weapons the antagonists found militarily useful, but development of new capabilities on a vast scale, including strategic aerial bombardment and global submarine warfare, rocket artillery, jet and rocket airplanes, flame throwers, incendiary bombs, jellied gasoline, radar, guided and ballistic missiles, and the atomic bomb. All major participants developed and stockpiled important gases and bacterial agents, the Germans making the most important breakthrough by inventing nerve gas. Large stocks of nerve gas were captured and stockpiled at war's end by both the United States and Russia, both of which are currently presumed to be pursuing intense chemical-biological weapons development programs. On the whole, the experience of World War II offered little on which to base serious hopes for the abandonment or limitation of armaments.

The search nevertheless continued, primarily under Articles 11, 26 and 47 of the United Nations Charter. Article 11 empowered the General Assembly to consider the problem and make recommendations to the members and the Security Council. Article 26 charged the Security Council with formulating plans to be submitted to the members, for establishment of a system for the regulation of armaments, and Article 47 established a Military Staff Committee to advise and assist the Security Council in this area. In 1946 the General Assembly created both an Atomic Energy Commission to control nuclear energy and

15

weapons, and a Commission on Conventional Armaments. Regulation of nuclear and nonnuclear arms was thus approached as two separate problems until 1952 when the two areas were combined under one agency, the Disarmament Commission. Between 1946 and 1952, little was accomplished by either agency, primarily because of Communist-Western disagreement over what constituted adequate procedures for inspection and regulation of development, production, deployment, and exchange of information. Generally, the Western powers demanded more detailed inspection than the Communist bloc was willing to allow, and the Communist members demanded more complete abandonment of nuclear weapons than the Western powers were willing to suffer.

Failing in its initial sessions, the Disarmament Commission in 1953 established a subcommittee, composed of representatives of the United States, the United Kingdom, the Soviet Union, France and Canada, to seek agreement through private meetings. The major differences between East and West persisted, however, and little was achieved. President Eisenhower's proposal at the Geneva Summit Conference in 1955, for an "open-skies" aerial inspection agreement to prevent surprise attack, was backed by an implementation plan submitted by the United States to the subcommittee, but negotiations became a tangle of detailed disputes over exactly which areas were to be open to inspection, and eventually ground to a halt in 1957. The Geneva recommendations on disarmament were also transmitted to the subcommittee, but met a similar fate. At Soviet insistence, the membership of the Disarmament Commission was broadened in 1958 to include all United Nations members, after which little was accomplished in that body.

In 1958, the United States and the Soviet Union convened groups of experts at Geneva to study the technical feasibility of detecting violations of a proposed nuclear test ban and of preventing surprise attack, but these talks foundered as a result both of technical difficulties and the West's refusal to discuss several issues presented by the Soviet Union on grounds that they were political, not technical. Despite this failure, the United States, the Soviet Union and the United Kingdom in 1958 joined in a voluntary nuclear test moratorium .

In 1959, the conference of Foreign Ministers at Geneva established a new committee of ten nations to consider disarmament questions. This led to the Ten Nations Disarmament Conference at Geneva in 1960, which failed when the Communist delegations walked out, claiming that the West refused to participate in substantive discussions. Also in 1959, the United Nations General Assembly unanimously approved the establishment of a permanent Committee on the Peaceful Uses of Outer Space. This new unit held its first meeting in 1961, after a two-year delay while disagreements over Soviet representation in the group's membership were being resolved. In 1963 the Committee initiated and secured the General Assembly's approval for a seventeen-nation resolution on the peaceful uses of outer space. The provisions of that resolution are embodied in the Space Treaty of 1967.

Discouragement and growing feelings of futility at disarmament efforts were intensified in 1960, when an anticipated U.S.-Soviet summit conference was canceled at the rocketing down over Russia of a U-2 spy plane, with which the United States had been practicing a unilateral "open-skies" program of its own. Only weeks later, the Soviets further deepened the gloom by violating the 1958 nuclear test moratorium with a series of nuclear explosions

17

to obtain large bomb data in the upper atmosphere and space.

Increasing apprehension as a result of these events, together with the Berlin and Cuban crises of 1961 and 1962, were major factors leading to the formation by the United States of a high-level Arms Control and Disarmament Agency to handle its negotiations, and the convening of the Seventeen Nations Disarmament Conference at Geneva in 1962. This conference has resulted in perhaps the most determined and massive efforts in history for arms control and disarmament. In conjunction with the United Nations, it hammered out the Limited Nuclear Test Ban Treaty of 1963, the Space Treaty of 1967, and the Nuclear Nonproliferation Treaty of 1968.

On the surface, these treaties may seem as monumental accomplishments, but one does not have to dig very far before getting a gnawing feeling that they represent little more than frustrated outward attempts at what is really, at least in the foreseeable future, unachievable. Two of the five current nuclear powers, Communist China and France have refused to participate either in the Conference or in any of its treaties, and Soviet sincerity in support of the test ban treaty must remain in doubt, in view of her deliberate violation of the 1958 test moratorium. Far more ominous, however, is the apparent unwillingness to sign the nonproliferation treaty, not only on the part of Red China and France, but of the dozen or more industralized nations approaching the capability to develop nuclear arms on their own within a few years. At this writing, none of the following nations had signed: Argentina, Australia, Brazil, Canada, Communist China, France, India, Indonesia, Israel, Italy, Japan, Mexico, Pakistan, Sweden, Switzerland, United Arab Republic, and West Germany. The nuclear nonproliferation treaty may be a desirable thing as a step toward reducing and, perhaps, preventing doomsday tensions, but there is little reason to believe that it will effectively halt the stockpiling of nuclear armament.

Currently, the strongest hopes for arms control are directed toward the Strategic Arms Limitation Talks (SALT) between the United States and the Soviet Union. A key to these talks would appear to be an effective moratorium on the development of MIRV which, if sufficiently accurate, would clearly be more of an aid to attack than to deterrence, and virtually impossible to detect without on-site inspection. Whether such a moratorium can be agreed, and if so, whether SALT can produce tangible results, can be seriously questioned in view of the degree to which MIRV developments have reportedly already proceeded. All factors considered, there unfortunately appear to be solid reasons, both historically and technically, for caution regarding the prospects for SALT.

Thus, the net result to date of all this tireless work has been demonstration of an almost total inability to control either the development or proliferation of increasingly destructive weapons. It is true that since World War I, the employment of gas and bacterial weapons has been generally avoided, except for their use by the Italians against Ethiopia in 1936 and by the Japanese against China in 1939. Much credit is surely due to President Roosevelt's announcement in 1943 that the Allies would not initiate their use. The motives behind this announcement probably were largely humanitarian, but many leaders are not restrained by such considerations. It cannot be doubted that if Hitler, for example, had found gas and bacterial weapons militarily practical and advantageous at the time, he would have used them against soldiers in battle as he did against civilians in concentration

19

camps. A primary reason for the avoidance of gas and bacterial warfare during the last half century is undoubtedly the risk of damage to one's own populations, which could result from unexpected wind and weather changes. The advent of nuclear weapons, however, with their equally destructive and unpredictable radioactive fallout effects, has done much to dilute the uniqueness of the risks associated with gas and bacteria, and their employment alongside nuclear weapons in any future strategic conflict must be accepted as a strong possibility.

After 150 years, it is painfully clear that even where arms control and disarmament have been truly desired, which itself was (and is) often questionable, there has been lacking the most critical necessary ingredient—mutual trust. Men have been willing to meet, debate, declare and even on occasion agree, endlessly, but no state has ever dared to make a first substantive move, fearful of the motives of others, and fearing that a resulting temporary condition of actual or apparent weakness would be exploited by someone else whose intentions were not so honorable.

All major powers without exception have raised this roadblock of mistrust at one time or another. American isolationism, German nationalism and Japanese imperialism lay behind the failures of the Hague Conferences, the League of Nations disarmament commissions, and the Washington, London and Geneva conferences of the 1930's. Communist expansionism and cold war suspicions, particularly on the part of the Soviets, have been largely responsible for the disappointing results of the United Nations commissions and the Geneva conferences since World War II. Currently, ancient hatred between Israel and the Arab states, and resurgent nationalism not only in France, China and apparently Japan but in scores of emerging nations, would seem to permit

20

little hope of preventing the proliferation of nuclear and other weapons of mass destruction. In such an environment, it is evident why no major state has yet dared a meaningful first step, and why such a step is improbable for generations at least.

The basic question has been confused by the fact that planners and diplomats, in their tenacity at pursuing the disarmament phantom, have managed over the years to produce a multitude of concepts for achieving the first critical step with acceptably small risk or loss of prestige. These myriad approaches, under many different names, are all only intricate variations on but a few central themes: the total renunciation of war, the partial renunciation of war, the prohibition of new arms development, the reduction of existing armaments, and the control of armaments by a supranational body.

The total renunciation of war was attempted on a formal basis in the 1928 Kellogg-Briand Pact; since then, its impracticality has been generally accepted and negotiators have confined their efforts to more realistic approaches. Following World War II, however, a similar attempt was made on a more limited-scale in the constitution forced upon Japan by the United States in 1946, Article 9 of which states that ". . . the Japanese people forever renounce war as a sovereign right of the nation and the threat or use of force as a means of settling disputes," and that ". . . land, sea and air forces will never be maintained." This constitution is still in effect, but because of the growing economic influence and independence of Japan, the rising tide of Japanese nationalist feeling, and her increasing predominance and interests in the Asian sphere, pressures appear to be mounting to cast off at least the shackle of Article 9. It seems only a matter of time before that occurs.

The partial renunciation of war has been attempted

21

in two primary modes: the renunciation of war in certain arenas made accessible by new delivery systems, and the renunciation of war involving certain classes of weapons.

Since the mid-nineteenth century, conventional armaments have been joined by four new kinds of weapons: chemical, including new methods for creating and distributing fire, gases both lethal and nonlethal, and psychochemicals; biological; nuclear, and radiological. Beginning with the Brussels Conference of 1874, various agreements have been reached prohibiting chemical and biological warfare. These proved ineffective in World War I, and relatively effective since then, but as stressed above the advent of nuclear weapons throws open the strong likelihood that chemical and biological warfare would be expected as part of any future nuclear conflict. Because of their unprecedented military value and entrenchment as a fact of life, no formal attempt has been made to outlaw nuclear weapons, and even the attempt to stem their proliferation appears to have been spurned, as noted above, by most of the nations immediately involved.

In the last century, four new arenas have been opened up by advancing technology, as theaters for military operations: the undersea, the atmosphere, the polar regions, and space. Numerous attempts have been made to declare all these arenas off-limits to military activities, including the 1899 Hague prohibition of submarines and balloon-launched projectiles, the 1932 U.S. proposals at Geneva to outlaw submarine warfare and bombing from aircraft, the Antarctic Treaty of 1959 banning mass destructive weapons and military bases there and, predictably, the Space Treaty of 1967 which did the same thing in regard to space. In 1969 both the United States and the Soviet Union have proposed in the United Nations, a treaty to prohibit the placement of nuclear weapons on the ocean floors.

22

The purpose of the Space Treaty is, of course, to preserve space as a largely demilitarized area in which peaceful activities can be conducted in a cooperative international basis, much as in Antarctica. The Soviets have long talked of this notion of demilitarized space, are party to the treaty, and give it lip service. Yet such talk must be regarded skeptically in view of ominous Soviet space developments, which will be discussed in Chapter IV, and in view of other statements which appear repeatedly in official Kremlin publications. For example, an article in *Krasnaya Zvezda* (Red Star), the newspaper of the Soviet Ministry of Defense, as reported in the *Los Angeles Times* (January 27, 1969), states that international exploration of space, as well as liquidation of the danger of wars, is impossible "so long as imperialism survives."

Like nuclear weapons, the undersea and atmospheric arenas are so fundamental in their strategic importance that all efforts at prohibiting military operations in these regions have been totally unsuccessful. To date, the Antarctic Treaty has been effective, but if the development of orbital bombardment systems should render delivery over the south polar regions militarily useful, then it is conceivable that pressures would mount for Antarctica to be utilized as a strategic theater, much as the Arctic serves as a basing region for advanced early warning systems against intercontinental bomber and missile attack.

The strategic implications of the space arena are only beginning to be dimly recognized. These implications and the increasingly military appearance of the Soviet national space program will be considered in some detail later. It is sufficient to say here that the general awakening to the strategic importance of space, especially since the announcement of FOBS less than one month after the Space Treaty went into effect, raises severe doubt whether space,

23

any more than the oceans or the atmosphere, can long be maintained off-limits to strategic forces.

Attempts to prohibit the development of new armaments have occurred several times when victors forced restrictive peaces on the vanquished, such as the Versailles Treaty imposed on Germany after World War I, and the unconditional surrender terms imposed on Germany and Japan at the close of World War II. The first binding international agreements of this sort were the 1958 Nuclear Test Moratorium which the Soviet Union broke in 1961, and the 1963 Limited Nuclear Test Ban Treaty. It should be noted that the main purpose of these agreements, however, was not to halt weapons development, which is permitted to continue more restrictively through underground testing, but to prevent worldwide radioactive contamination of the atmosphere.

Indirect efforts to discourage new weapons development have included unilateral restraint by the United States from development of thermonuclear bombs and intercontinental missiles in the 1950's, and military space systems in the 1960's, until such moves were forced upon the United States by Soviet initiatives. More recently, the Nuclear Nonproliferation Treaty of 1968 sought to achieve mutual agreements to prevent proliferation of nuclear weapons by development, purchase or military aid to allies or satellites. The dim prospects for this treaty have already been noted.

Thus, neither the direct nor indirect approaches cited above have been able to halt or even slow significantly the development and proliferation of mass destructive weapons, and neither shows any promise of better success in the future. Actually, attempts at prohibiting new armament development may ignore an important potential source of hope, namely, that the threat to humanity comes mainly from the accumulation of present armaments, and that new weapons might offer the only realistic possibilities of creating new situations wherein this threat could be reduced.

Proposals for freezing, reducing or gradually eliminating existing armaments have abounded. These include the 1908–1914 Anglo-German negotiations on reduction of naval expenditures, the Versailles Treaty, various League of Nations commissions, the naval conferences of the 1920's and 1930's, and several U.S. and Soviet proposals following World War II. Virtually nothing of importance has been achieved, since this approach is subject to all the obstacles noted above, particularly Soviet reluctance at the prospect of establishing inspection and enforcement to mutual satisfaction, and the reluctance of any state to make a first critical move. The United States perhaps came closest when it unilaterally reduced its armed forces by over 90 percent after World War II, only to regret this at the time of the first Soviet nuclear test in 1949 and the outbreak of the Korean conflict in 1950.

The placing of armaments under the control of a supranational agency has been widely discussed, but seldom seriously considered as a practical objective, since it is virtually impossible to imagine foolproof or fail-safe organizational machinery to prevent undue influence or seizure of that agency by unscrupulous interests. Few situations whet the appetites of potential dictators, nor are more subject to their usurpation, than great power highly concentrated. It is a question of who is going to watch the watchman.

This history of almost total failure is discouraging even to the most confirmed optimist, because it is convincing evidence that all forms of arms control, reduction or liquidation, depend fundamentally on a degree of mutual trust still not in sight. Many negotiations are based on the hope that some form of inspection agreement can be found to compensate for this lack of trust, but this seems remote. Even aside from political considerations, practical problems alone present formidable obstacles to maintenance of sufficient surveillance over the internal activities of an industrial society, to render feasible the detection of development and production of weapons and delivery systems. This is especially true of chemical and biological agents, which require only small and inconspicuous facilities such as chemical processing plants and common breweries. It is also true of delivery systems such as ships, aircraft and space vehicles, in which differences between military and nonmilitary versions can be made slight, convertibility easy, and the problems of effective inspection very complex.

After a century and a half of searching for arms control and disarmament agreements, surely the time has come to recognize that the prospects for success in the foreseeable future are distressingly thin. This is not to admit ultimate failure, since there must still be hope as long as anything remains untried, and because any level of agreement at all in this area may contribute to peace by relieving tensions in some measure. But it is unavoidable that in the light of what they have produced so far, such agreements do not yet promise sufficiently solid foundations to any power, for realistic policy footings where national security is at stake.

POPULATION, WAR AND THE FUTILITY OF CIVIL DEFENSE

Aside from onrushing weapons technology, there is another seemingly irresistible force which must intensify

26

not only the consequences, but the probability, of conflict: the accelerating growth and patterns of world population. Within the next century or so, barring large-scale war and worldwide population control, at least fifty billion new human beings may be expected on earth, a number equal to all the people who have been born since the pyramids were built, and about half the number who have ever lived on the planet since the beginnings of man millions of years ago.

How far technical progress in the production of food, materials and energy can go in sustaining these masses of humanity has been debated inconclusively, but estimates of the maximum world population which could be supported using conceivable techniques of enhanced productivity and marine agriculture range up to and even beyond fifty billion. If these technologies do advance in such a rapid manner—and certainly history allows us to be optimistic about such progress—then there may be perhaps a century or so of grace in which to solve the birth control problem before world population growth eventually does overtake the supply of food and other resources. Provided, of course, that present disparities in food output such as between the United States and India can be alleviated by imported agriculture and equitable distribution.

Within this period of grace, therefore, despite chronic food shortages in certain areas of Asia which have existed for long periods of time, the threat of catastrophic war appears far more immediate that that of world starvation. Indeed, the growth of population itself and its patterns of distribution are factors which expand the likelihood and compound the probable consequences of war.

In 1900, world population was about 1.6 billion, in 1950 about 2.5 billion, and by the year 2000 it is ex-

27

pected to swell to between 5 and 7 billion. Thus, the latter half of the twentieth century should see world population increase by 2.5 to 4.5 billion people. Of this increase, about 85 percent will be added outside North America, Europe and the Soviet Union, in areas where living standards are low but hope and envy run high. With this population expansion, it is doubtful whether technology and industrialization, even augmented by foreign aid, can do more than merely maintain living standards in these areas, much less raise them. Meanwhile, the industrial nations will continue to improve their lot, so that by the year 2000 the United States probably will control nearly half the world's wealth with only five percent of the world's population. North America, Europe, the Soviet Union and Japan can be expected to account for 85 percent of world output, with less than 25 percent of world population.

Mounting unrest arising from these causes can only sharpen the probability of wars. The outlook becomes even more ominous in view of the fact that these great population explosions and problems of living standards will loom primarily among the nonwhite races, especially in China, India, Africa and Latin America. Because of the depth of racial antagonisms and mistrust which have always existed and seem unlikely to mellow soon, it is difficult to overemphasize the significance of the increasing numerical dominance of the colored races. This is especially relevant in regard to Communist China, where memories of oppression by Caucasians, present hostile attitudes and rising nuclear capability, cast a forbidding shadow across the future.

Future populations will be increasingly vulnerable to the effects of war, as a result of the flow of people into swelling cities, which has always accompanied industrialization and must be expected to continue with further technological and industrial progress. In the United States in 1960, nearly 50 percent of the people were clustered in the hundred largest cities, up from 30 percent ten years earlier. In contrast, the corresponding percentages for the Soviet Union in 1959 and for Communist China are only about 20 percent and 10 percent respectively. The high susceptibility to nuclear attack, of urbanized populations, is thus forcefully evident especially in the United States where, it may be added, 70 percent of the population is concentrated in just over one percent of the land area.

Protection of city populations from the effects of nuclear warfare, both by active defense in the form of interceptor missiles and passive defense such as fallout shelters, as well as combinations of the two, has been intensively studied and debated in the United States, and presumably elsewhere. The technical feasibiliy of city defense by antimissile missiles, especially against ballistic missile salvo attacks, appears very doubtful, and a national program of fallout shelters has never received active support, perhaps partly because history has shown that defense schemes based on extensive static facilities on the surface or underground, such as the Maginot Line, rapidly become obsolete and contribute little to new technology. Further, nuclear fallout shelters probably would be quite useless to protect against penetration by other weapons such as gases and bacterial clouds.

The eventual decision in 1967 to deploy the U.S. Sentinel antimissile system against possible light attacks, without accompanying fallout shelters, and the shifting of this system in 1969 under the new name Safeguard, to defense of strategic missile sites only, appear to rule out expectation of a shelter program on an extensive basis. In general, the technical problems of protecting concentrated populations against massive coordinated missile attacks such as could now be launched by either the Soviet Union or the United States, and foreseeably by Communist China and France, are so difficult as to have been officially acknowledged as insurmountable. On November 3, 1967, Secretary of Defense McNamara publicly admitted, "There is no way on earth to defend U.S. cities." It must be presumed that this holds for all the other cities of the world as well.

To what degree and how, then, could it be hoped that civilian populations might be spared catastrophe in event of a nuclear war? There seems to be nothing inherent in the nature of war that makes the destruction of noncombatants necessary or even militarily desirable as a general rule. Four basic kinds of tragedies have befallen populations in wartime, arguments for the military necessity of which are tenuous indeed.

First, where war is expected to last long enough to require military equipment produced after it starts, as well as that in being at the outset, segments of the populace and economy may be considered important targets inasmuch as they contribute to the war effort. In World War II, however, which was protracted and in which civilian production and morale were critical elements, the military value of strategic city bombing remains doubtful after detailed evaluation in retrospect. Hitler's diversion of the Luftwaffe from its successful attacks against R.A.F. installation to the population bombing of London, and the Allied raids which ruined Berlin, Hamburg, Dresden, Tokyo, Hiroshima and Nagasaki, can be regarded as having produced little of military value compared to their destructiveness. The two atomic raids did end the war, perhaps saving more lives on both sides than they took, but it seems probable now, and did then to many in-

30

formed individuals, that the same result could have been accomplished by demonstration bursts over uninhabited areas or the ocean. More recently, the apparent ineffectiveness of the American bombing campaign against North Veitnam, seems to add credibility to these conclusions.

Second, whole populations have been liquidated for political, racial or religious reasons. From a military viewpoint this is absurd, since it not only destroys potentially useful human resources, but wastefully diverts manpower and material. Nonetheless, military activity has served as a cover for mass extermination from the times of Alexander and Caesar, whose atrocities though often forgotten were not minor, to those of Stalin, Hitler and Mao.

A third kind of war-caused population disaster is starvation and disease, which have generally not been military objectives but rather unwanted by-products of warfare. It killed 25 million in the Black Death of 1347–1350, the result of a Tartar raid in the Crimea, at least 10 million during the Napoleonic Wars, and nearly 20 million in the influenza epidemic of 1918–1919. Fortunately, medical advances greatly reduced pestilence and starvation during World War II, but at the same time increased man's understanding and control of these forces so that chemical and biological weapons now form a lethal branch of military technology which could be brought to bear on a global scale in a future war.

Fourth, military systems have been deployed so close to populated centers that collateral damage could not be avoided, and attacks on the military were in effect attacks on the populace and economy as well. This is one of the most frightening aspects of the nuclear age, since the destructiveness of nuclear weapons is so great that attacks on even military installations alone, wherever on earth they are located, could spread blast, thermal and fallout destruction across much of the planet's population. The deployment of strategic systems across homeland areas and among civilian populations has been described as the act of holding one's own people hostage. While perhaps offering advantages of low cost and simplicity, this can hardly be justified morally, however convinced one may be that this hostage game will deter a potential attacker. As long as the strategic forces of the major powers are confined to the earth as a deployment and operational arena, this situation is inescapable.

History, therefore, gives little reason to believe that actual destruction of civil populations is ever an intrinsic military necessity. Since the development of nuclear and biological weapons, however, when technology conferred the capability to threaten populations with instant and total destruction, the power and availability of this kind of *threat* would appear to have established it as a more or less permanent fact of life. There appears no way to ensure that the threat and even occasional use of counterpopulace attack can be absolutely avoided forever, either in the cause of deterrence or more sinister objectives. The only realistic recourse, aside from continuous efforts to avoid nuclear tragedy through wise policy and diplomacy, would appear to be determined pursuit of:

First, strengthened deterrence, especially through maintaining and improving the survivability of strategic systems. In this regard the current value of ocean based systems is evident, as well as the increasing potential of space-based systems, as ships and submarines inevitably become more vulnerable to detection and attack.

Second, counterforce capability, to dilute motivations and fears of population attack. Here, it might be objected that counterforce is of main value to an attacker as a means of reducing his opponent's retaliatory force in a surprise strike, rather than to a deterrent power, since it might seem unlikely that an attacker having made his first strike, would allow his remaining forces to sit as targets for the expected retaliatory blow. There is some strength to this point of view, but the counterarguments are equally strong. First, there is no guarantee that a future war will take the form of a simple all-out strike-retaliation or one-two exchange of blows. Second, counterforce capability on the deterrent side tends to restrict the variety of strategies open to the attacker, as well as permitting more flexible response to a wider range of eventualities, such as tit-for-tat exchanges with evaluation and bargaining periods interspersed.

Third, more distant deployment of strategic systems, to alleviate the threat of collateral damage to populations, from attacks on military installations. Here again, the potential of space-based systems begins to become apparent.

And fourth, brief war capability, to reduce further the motivations and fears of attacks on the populace and economy.

These four objectives are of varying difficulty and may not all be achievable to the degree which might be hoped. They appear sufficiently realistic, however, and of sufficient importance to a deterrent power such as the United States, that if their pursuit is not undertaken with great energy it could well be overtaken by grave events.

FORTRESS EARTH AND ARMAGEDDON

Throughout the world there are growing stockpiles of mass destructive weapons and global delivery systems more than adequate to end civilization and life on the planet, if they are ever released against earthbound targets.

33

The word "overkill" has become an everyday part of our vocabulary. How likely they are to be used eventually, may depend heavily on how many powers come to control them, and the dangers of the spread of nuclear weapons are justly the source of current intense and apprehensive diplomatic efforts toward a nonproliferation treaty. Even if ratification of such a treaty were achieved, there are strong reasons as noted above to think that the treaty will be ineffective in the longer run, because it does not appear to have the support of all the present, let alone potential, nuclear powers.

Even if proliferation could be halted, and nuclear weapons were restricted to the present "club" consisting of the United States, the Soviet Union, Britain, France and Communist China, then if there were only one chance in 100,000 each day that any one of these states were to start a nuclear exchange either accidentally, by miscalculation or irresponsibility, then accumulating probabilities would render nuclear war a virtual certainty in less than fifty years.

This period is shortened if one allows the more likely case of acquisition of nuclear armaments by any of the several previously mentioned nations potentially capable of this by, say, 1980. It is further shortened if one allows for additional complications arising from the spread of chemical and biological warfare capabilites, which fall within the technical and industrial capacities of many nations. In addition, it is conceivable that by use of small-scale underground testing techniques, certain nations may be able to develop nuclear weapons secretly, in which case the political situation could not be evaluated properly by the rest of the world, and a miscalculated nuclear war might be touched off by a surprise move from a hitherto unsuspected or unidentified quarter.

A scenario along these lines is imaginable. It might begin with Israel secretly developing a nuclear weapons technology, testing underground when necessary at some remote site in the Sinai Peninsula. Impressed with the advantages of surprise which had been demonstrated in the war of June, 1967, by which it had acquired the Sinai, Israel might decide for its own preservation to follow similar policies in the future, but with the additional confidence of its secret nuclear power. The Arab world, fearing this, might in desperation begin to purchase nuclear know-how and materials from Communist China, France, or any other power not participating in the Nuclear Nonproliferation Treaty.

Realities even more sobering are becoming apparent. As the nuclear power industry spreads, shipments of nuclear materials increase and it is becoming more difficult to guard such shipments adequately against hijacking. This has led the chairman of the Atomic Energy Commission to concede, as reported in *The Wall Street Journal* (June 13, 1968), that a black market in nuclear materials could develop. Such a black market, combined with increasingly available information about firing devices, could place nuclear weapons in the hands not only of many smaller nations, but of insurrectionists, terrorists and criminals as well.

Nuclear proliferation on these levels would only hasten the day when a large-scale war could be touched off, especially if great-power deterrence had become unstable.

In the United States, the mid-century armaments race has resulted in the basing of a growing percentage of our strategic nuclear delivery and missile defense systems, within the length and breadth of our continental land mass. These systems must be considered prime potential targets in any nuclear attack, and in such an event their deployment throughout the country would result in wind-borne radioactive fallout blanketing most of the nation, even if cities were not attacked directly. This is creating a Fortress America, in which the entire population would be swept up in the holocaust of a strategic exchange. The same kinds of systems are being rushed in the Soviet Union, France, and can be expected in Communist China, so that the pattern extends and proliferates, bringing closer the dark reality of Fortress Earth.

It is frequently asserted that the deterrent effect of these homeland-based systems is so great that no rational, responsible leader would dare an attack. Even if this is true, it is academic in that leaders are not always rational or responsible in their actions, no one is immune to accident or miscalculation, and the probabilities associated with these contingencies cannot be measured neatly in mathematical terms. Whether the button is pushed by accident, miscalculation or irresponsibility, and when, will be of little consequence to those left afterward.

Further justification for apprehension about the future, if it were needed, could be obtained from studies which show that in recent history there has been an alarming increase not only in the total number of people killed in wars, but also the percentage of world population killed per decade.* In the twelfth century, available statistics indicate, average war casualties were 0.2 per thousand of world population per decade, which had gradually increased to about 2.0 per thousand by the end of the eighteenth century. Since the Industrial Revolution, however, this figure had shot upward to about 20 per thousand, and in that 200-year period, war deaths had swelled

*L. F. Richardson, *Statistics of Deadly Quarrels* (Pittsburgh: Boxwood Press, 1966).

from about 0.2 to about 3 per thousand. It is emphasized that these increases are almost entirely the result of advances in conventional weaponry only. While V-2 ballistic missiles and two atomic bombs were used near the end of World War II, their contribution to total war dead was negligible.

In any future large-scale wars on earth, the use of ballistic and orbital rockets and nuclear, chemical and biological weapons must be anticipated with expanded human and material damage. When this might occur, from what causes and under what circumstances, can only be surmised. If these historical trends are continued, however, even allowing for natural population growth, it can be shown that within little more than another century, humanity will have been totally extinguished. The accident, miscalculation or irresponsibility need occur only once again.

A straight look at reality must thus lead to a hard view of the future, to anyone sufficiently honest with himself to separate hopes from facts. The hopes are that men will acquire before it is too late the mutual trust and common sense to avoid arms races and large-scale wars. The facts are: that deep-rooted self-interested motivations leading to conflict and war, appear not yet subject to rational control; that the increase and distribution of man's own numbers are in themselves powerful factors leading to war; and that in large-scale war, it must be anticipated that all classes of weapons will be used—weapons which have reached a stage of development where civil population can no longer be spared devastation, even from side effects.

The probable consequences of running deeper the old ruts of reliance on earthbound weapons races, disarmament, and futile attempts at missile defense, should by now be evident. A new possibility rapidly coming within our technical grasp is to extend our deterrent forces to space rather than concentrating them in Fortress America, Fortress Russia or Fortress China. In this perspective, it is hard to see how we can responsibly continue to avoid giving serious attention to that increasingly clear alternative.

This is not to diminish in any way the critical importance of more protracted attempts to improve world conditions through tenacious efforts at promoting trade, education, improved living standards and population and even arms control. Work in these areas may produce a real source of hope for the long run. This hope does not, however, solve the immediately looming question of how to survive within a system of strategic balances which grow less steady each year.

Since experience so strongly suggests that it will be a long time before we lay our weapons aside or be willing to accept diplomatic limitations on our basic military capabilities as nations, then survival itself will depend heavily on access to arenas of battle wide enough that we may somehow avoid self-destruction. Until recently those arenas could be in the plains, mountains and seas at relatively safe distances from towns and cities. In the nuclear age, however, such earthbound margins of safety are no longer adequate, and it could develop that our only real hope for survival is that space will provide the battlefields, in a time when arms and war have outgrown the planet.

II

PROMISE BEYOND THE SKY

Our earth is but a small star in the great universe.
Yet of it we can make, if we choose, a planet unvexed by war.
FRANKLIN D. ROOSEVELT

In the nuclear age, space is a natural battlefield. Its potential as an arena for strategic forces can be fully appreciated only if one obtains first a grasp of its immensity, which is such as to dwarf the destructive scales of even the largest nuclear weapons, and swallow up the most extensive military operations.

To illustrate the scale of this arena, imagine the earth to be the size of a basketball. The sky, or the navigable portion of the atmosphere, extends up to less than one tenth of an inch above the surface of the ball. Above the atmosphere lies near-orbit space, up to the inner reaches of the Van Allen radiation belt about three quarters of an inch above the surface. The strongest portions of this radiation belt taper off something like five feet further outward. Beyond is far-orbit space which reaches to the extremities of the earth's gravitational dominance 40 to 50 feet away in all directions, and within which the moon circles its orbit at a distance of about 26 feet. Further still are the vast stretches of interplanetary space, where Venus and Mars in their orbits never swing closer than 2500 and 3600 feet respectively, the sun is nearly two miles away, and the planet Pluto at the outer edge of the solar system ranges out to distances up to ninety miles. The nearest star, Alpha Centauri, is about five *million* miles away, even on this tiny scale.

On this scale, a 20-megaton warhead, such as the one referred to previously as representative of what may be mounted on the Soviet SS-9 intercontinental missiles, would burn out a lethal sphere three quarters of an inch in diameter, if burst in space. A lethal sphere the size of the basketball "earth" itself, would be generated by a 10,000-megaton bomb, a weapon which probably could be built with today's technology. Much smaller bursts could contaminate all near-orbit space and most of the Van Allen Belt when account is taken of the ability of the earth's magnetic field to trap nuclear-burst particles and disperse them through the span of the belt. Thus, even looking beyond the earth and considering neighboring space in the vicinity of the earth's magnetic field, it is apparent that here, too, is a region which is still small by nuclear standards and which could be saturated readily with destructive radiation in event of a nuclear war.

When space is viewed in the broadening perspectives of lunar and interplanetary scales, however, then even the largest nuclear bursts begin to dwindle to insignificance. Beyond lunar space, the earth's gravitational influence extends some half million miles or more before fading into interplanetary space where solar gravity begins to predominate, and there is nothing to preclude operations from solar orbits where vehicles would describe slow looping patterns with respect to the earth, always staying somewhere within a few million miles. As described later, the energy requirements for reaching such distances are essentially no greater than for climbing out of the Van Allen belt, the primary penalty being only the times necessary to coast across such great stretches.

In these volumes, in which distances are measured in millions of miles, the largest nuclear bursts are no more than pebble splashes in an ocean. Even if some future technology should result in further increases in weapon destructive scales, still space has practically no effective limits. It stretches on to distances taxing the imagination, to include not only the sun and planets, but interstellar voids which lie beyond, and then farther still. Space is an arena so vast that it could contain and insulate any form of warfare conceivable in the context of the physical sciences.

This raises the central question: *Is it possible that*

42

the space arena may promise sufficient military advantages to motivate both deterrent and potentially aggressive powers to extend their strategic capabilities to space, so that perhaps there eventually might result, as a natural consequence, a progressive reduction of earthbound strategic stockpiles, and a lessening of the expected levels of violence on earth in event of a nuclear war?

WAR IN SPACE AND PEACE ON EARTH?

There are sound reasons to think, as emphasized previously, that attacks on populations are in most cases not inherently necessary or even desirable from a military viewpoint, particularly if strategic systems are survivable, counterforce capability exists, and the war is expected to be sufficiently short so that operations do not depend heavily on post-attack production capacity or civilian morale. Even after thorough study, the military value of the city attacks in World War II, which was a protracted conflict, remains doubtful at best. Most population mortalities in recent wars, have resulted from the collateral damage, disease and starvation arising primarily from the *proximity* of war.

It should not be pretended that extension and perhaps eventual removal of at least some strategic forces to space would eliminate population targeting, but in the event that deterrence failed and a nuclear exchange did occur, it almost certainly would:

(a) Reduce the total nuclear yield expected to be exploded in the atmosphere, with consequent reduction in expected world fallout.

(b) Reduce thus the risk of unleashing chemical and biological war.

43

(c) Reduce also the risk of widespread collateral damage, disease and starvation.

(d) Increase the political difficulty to a potential aggressor who targeted populations without even the partial excuse of nearby bomber, missile or submarine bases.

(e) Alleviate the moral problem of holding one's own populations hostage.

The question may be asked whether it would make sense to extend military systems to space when the prizes of war, or objects of control, are human and material resources back on earth. The primary purpose of strategic force delivery systems is not to occupy territory, but to destroy the enemy's own strategic forces and resources. Occupation requires ground troops and is beyond the purpose or capability of bombers, submarines and missiles, independent of the locations from which they are launched. In this sense, bombardment from space is no different than bombardment from earth. The degree to which military occupation would even be required in connection with a future war may be open to question. If, for example, the Soviets could in any manner destroy or negate the American strategic weapons systems, then they would be relatively free to extend their sphere of influence, even if few Soviets ever set foot in the United States, which then might be expected gradually to wither as a world power.

Conflicts are ultimately decided by threats or contests between strategic systems regardless of their location. Before the advent of bombers and missiles, strategic systems consisted of masses of infantry which battled each other directly, occupation being in a sense incidental to gaining access and controlling the enemy's strategic force, and a result of the fact that masses of foot soldiers are confined

44

to someone's land surface as an arena, usually their own, the enemy's, or that of some unfortunate people caught in between.

As technology has shifted primary strategic dependence from the land-bound infantry to devices which operate in other arenas, conflicts in distant places have become increasingly important in helping decide the courses of wars. History provides many examples of decisive battles often unseen by noncombatants, including the Greek naval victory over the Persians at the battle of Salamis (480 B.C.), the defeat of the Spanish Armada (1588), the Battle of Britain (1940), and all the battles in jungles, on islands, across deserts, on and beneath the oceans and in the sky, since then. Few such contests have of themselves decided the outcomes of wars, because in the past, armies, navies and air forces have each formed only fractions of the total strategic force mix. The advance of technology, however, has tended to shift a growing portion of strategic reliance, first from ground and naval forces to bombers, then gradually to missiles, such that in a future war a missile exchange could be decisive, regardless whether it involves earth-to-earth, space-to-earth, or space-to-space encounters.

It would thus seem reasonable to expect that the more a strategic conflict could be made to occur in space, the less probable would be an all-consuming holocaust on earth. How, then, could strategic capabilities be extended to space? The history of arms control and disarmament gives little reason to hope that this could be achieved by direct diplomatic means. The remaining question is whether we dare hope that such an extension, and perhaps eventual transition, could be expected to occur naturally as a result of inherent strategic benefits of operating in the space arena.

There appear to be several reasons to hold such hopes,

45

which can be clarified only by investigating specific military implications and potential benefits of strategic space operations for both deterrent and aggressive powers. In order to do this, it is first necessary to survey briefly the characteristics of the space arena itself.

REGIONS OF THE SPACE ARENA

Space is not a featureless void, but is filled with dynamic phenomena such as matter, gravitational and magnetic fields, and radiation. The patterns of these phenomena define distinct regions, each having its own potential operational and military implications. On earth the land, sea and air arenas are composed of regions set apart by particular combinations of conditions such as surface composition and characteristics, altitude or depth, temperature and rainfall. Similarly, the space arena consists of operational regions defined by the distribution of matter, gravitational and magnetic field strength, and radiation intensity. The following discussion outlines the more important of these regions in terms of their size, energy and radiation environments and the characteristics of motion within them, as well as some miltary implications which suggest themselves more or less immediately.

Within the predominant gravitational influence of the earth, space can be divided into the following four regions: near orbit, magnetosphere, far-orbit and lunar.

Near-orbit space is that region lying immediately above the outer-portions of the earth's atmosphere and extending to the inner fringes of the Van Allen trapped radiation belt. It reaches from roughly 100 miles to an average of about 600 miles altitude, forming a roughly spherical shell enclosing the earth, and containing over

46

100 billion cubic miles. This compares with a volume of about 20 billion cubic miles for the entire atmosphere, less than 15 billion of which contain air of sufficient density to serve as an arena for aerodynamic operations. Near-orbit space is therefore about five to seven times the size of the atmospheric arena.

Because the earth's magnetic axis is tilted nearly 20 degrees from its geographic axis, and does not run exactly through the center of the globe, the terrestrial magnetic field is slightly asymmetric in relation to the earth, so that the magnetically trapped radiation forming the Van Allen Belt dips well below its average bottom altitude of 600 nautical miles, at a point in the South Atlantic Ocean just off the east coast of Argentina. The outer boundary of near-orbit space is thus not at constant altitude, but varies continuously from place to place and its low region, called the South Atlantic Anomaly, can present hazards to manned near-orbit vehicles in that area. Even at natural levels, some Van Allen radiation at the anomaly extends as low as the ionosphere, although this condition is tolerable for unshielded manned vehicles. If the belt is augmented by electrons from a nuclear burst, however, the radiation intensities at the anomaly can easily be raised to levels intolerable to even heavily shielded vehicles. Further, as already mentioned, this condition may last for years.

Although the Van Allen Belt thus may impose large shielding penalties on manned vehicles, it actually provides shielding against the high-energy proton radiation emanating sporadically from disturbances on the sun called solar flares. Because of the focusing effect of the earth's magnetic field, these proton bursts are funneled around the Van Allen Belt and pass downward through near-orbit space to enter the atmosphere in the polar regions. Near-orbit vehicles are thus shielded from solar flares so long as they remain under the Van Allen Belt, which extends in latitude from approximately 45 degrees north to 45 degrees south. Near-orbit manned vehicles operating outside these limits, in polar or near-polar orbits, must avoid flights during solar flares, carry solar-flare shielding, or be prepared to return to earth immediately upon occurrence of a flare.

Being the strongest region of the earth's gravitational field, near-orbit space is characterized by high orbital velocities, in the neighborhood of 25,000 feet per second, so that any vehicles in near orbits perform complete circuits of the earth within about 90 to 110 minutes. Such high velocities make in-space maneuvering exceedingly difficult. Although changes in orbital altitude may be made with moderate propulsion weight penalties, any turns or plane changes greater than a few degrees are essentially impractical without nuclear propulsion and even then are very costly. Because of this, near-orbital vehicles have little capability to deviate from their predicted paths which, because of their nearness to the earth, can be readily detected and determined in detail by hostile ground stations after only a few orbital passes.

This restriction can be eased somewhat by providing the vehicle with propulsion and aerodynamic surfaces to enable it to deorbit to the atmosphere, perform its maneuvers aerodynamically in the outer layers of rarified air, and then either return to earth or climb back to establish a new orbit. This kind of operation, however, is advantageous for very low orbits only, and even then the required propulsion and structural weights impose significant penalties on the vehicles space-operating capabilities, so that aerodynamic maneuverng may be practical only for special types of near-orbit operations, such as, perhaps, dash missions for reconnaissance.

48

The second region of space, the magnetosphere, is that region lying immediately outside near-orbit space and extending to include the inner and strongest portions of the earth's magnetic field. This region has the property of trapping radiations from the sun and space in a dough-nut-shaped volume centered roughly around the earth's equator between the approximate latitudes of 45 degrees north and 45 degrees south. This volume is filled pre-dominately with high-energy protons in the inner portions and low-energy electrons in its outer reaches. These trapped radiations constitute the Van Allen Belt, which extends outward 25,000 to 60,000 miles depending on solar flare conditions. If 60,000 miles is taken as the maxi-mum altitude of the magnetosphere, then this region of space is seen to form an appropriately spherical shell en-closing both the earth and near-orbit space, and contain-ing over 900 thousand billion cubic miles, or about 9,000 times the volume of near-orbit space.

Actually, the magnetosphere is not a sphere at all, but a region resembling a comet in shape with the earth located in the head, and a tail sweeping away from the sun to lunar distances and beyond. The inner portions within 60,000 miles of the earth, however, will be referred to here as the magnetosphere, because of the potential practical implications of their far stronger fields.

The polar sections of the magnetosphere not occupied by the Van Allen Belt, though free of intense trapped radiation, have the property already noted, of funneling solar and space radiations down to the Arctic and Ant-arctic regions. The magnetosphere is thus composed of an equatorial section filled with continuous Van Allen radiations, and two polar sections characterized by inter-mittent pulses of solar flare radiation. At natural levels, the radiation intensities in the inner portions of the Van Allen Belt prohibit stay-times greater than about thirty

49

minutes for unshielded manned vehicles, and heavy shielding penalties are required to remain there safely for longer periods. Fortunately, however, trajectories to far-orbit space, the moon or beyond, require less than thirty minutes to traverse the approximately 6,000-mile thickness of the proton region, so that transfer missions to deep space do not require shielding for Van Allen Belt pass-through. The electron intensities in the outer portions of the Van Allen Belt present less severe hazards, and relatively light shielding can enable manned vehicles to remain there indefinitely, aside from solar flare effects.

The entire belt, however, probably can be rendered not only uninhabitable but impassable, by an appropriately located nuclear burst or bursts of only moderate size. Such an action could have the effect of limiting manned access not only to near-orbit space, as already mentioned, and the Van Allen Belt itself, but also to deep space if Van Allen pass-through is required. Access to deep space would be restricted to the polar volumes of the magnetosphere, and since these serve also as funnels for sporadic bursts of extremely intense solar flare particle streams, use of them as "gateways to space" would impose additional requirements for solar flare predictions and launch timing, and especially launch site location and vehicle maneuverability.

Since it occupies a weaker region of the earth's gravitational field than near-orbit space, the magnetosphere is characterized by lower orbital velocities and longer orbital periods. Circular orbit velocities range from 25,000 feet per second at the inner extremity, to just over 10,000 feet per second in synchronous 24-hour orbit at 22,300 miles altitude, to 7,000 feet per second at 60,000 miles altitude. The corresponding periods are 110 minutes, 24 hours, and about 3.2 days.

50

Beyond the magnetosphere is a region which will be referred to as far-orbit space. It is a spherical shell extending out to a distance of roughly 600,000 or more miles, and within which the earth's gravitational influence still predominates. It contains more than 750 million billion cubic miles, about 8,500 times the volume of the magnetosphere and 7.5 million times that of near-orbit space.

Because this region includes the weakest reaches of the terrestrial gravitational field, it is characterized by orbital velocities much lower and orbital periods much longer than those associated with either near-orbit space or the magnetosphere. At its inner extremities, say 60,000 miles altitude, circular orbit velocity and period are 7,000 feet per second and 3.2 days. At the lunar distance of about 230,000 miles, they are 3,500 feet per second and of course 28 days, and ideally at 600,000 miles they would be 2,000 feet per second and 91 days, if no account were taken of the effects of solar gravity, which at such distances begins to predominate.

The relatively low orbital velocities associated with far-orbit space permits a wide variety of maneuvers with reasonably small propulsion weight penalties, once the price has been paid to climb into this region. It is, for example, not unrealistic to think of a vericle in far-orbit being capable of constantly changing its orbit to complicate the problem of detection and tracking by the enemy, which in far-orbit space is formidable in any case because of the great distances and small visual angles involved. Indeed, at distances comparable to or greater than that of the moon, where solar gravitational effects become increasingly significant, the combined effects of the terrestrial, lunar and solar gravities cause vehicular orbits to be skewed into meanderings which are difficult to predict anyway, even in the absence of powered maneuvers.

51

The interaction of the earth's and moon's gravitational fields creates in far-orbit space five points, called libration points, at which vehicles can remain stationary with respect to the earth and moon. Three of these points lie along the earth-moon axis, the first being about 192,000 miles from the earth between the earth and moon at the point where the two gravitational fields are equal in strength. The second lies about 36,000 miles beyond the moon, and the third lies about 230,000 miles from earth on the side away from the moon. The fourth and fifth, or "equilateral," points lie in the moon's orbit, respectively preceding and following it in its motion around the earth, by 60 degrees of arc in either case.

In the absence of other gravitational fields, vehicles at any of the first three points are in unstable equilibrium, so that propulsion is required to maintain their position in case of any disturbing forces, while vehicles at the equilateral points are stable, such that any disturbing forces result in natural restoring forces coming into play. Actually, the effects of solar gravity and non-circularity of the moon's orbit increase the tendency toward instability in all five points, although vehicles can be kept near the equilateral points for long periods for only minimal propulsion penalties. The libration points thus suggest themselves as likely locations for surveillance vehicles, especially when the objects of surveillance are on or near the moon.

Being beyond the strong magnetosphere, far-orbit space is free from continuous radiations except for the weak regions of the magnetospheric tail and low-level background particles from the sun and cosmos, but is subject to very high-intensity particle streams thrown out intermittently by solar flares. Manned vehicles operating for periods greater than a few days must therefore carry solar-flare shielding, although shuttle missions between the earth and any point in far-orbit space can be accomplished in no more than hours or days and can probably avoid this weight penalty.

Lunar space is that region in which the lunar gravitational field is predominant. It extends from the lunar surface out to a boundary which is roughly egg-shaped, the long end pointing toward earth and terminating at the first libration point about 37,000 miles from the earth-facing lunar surface. Lunar space contains over 45 thousand billion cubic miles, equivalent to more than 450 times the volume of near-orbit space but only about 0.06 of one percent of the volume of far-orbit space.

Because the lunar gravitational field is relatively weak, lunar space is characterized by relatively slow orbital velocities, ranging from 5,500 feet per second near the lunar surface to perhaps 1,000 feet per second at the outer boundary of the region. The corresponding orbital periods range from about 110 minutes near the surface to approximately one week near the outer boundary. As in the case of far orbits, these low velocities open up possibilities for appreciable vehicle maneuvers with reasonable propulsion weights. Access to the lunar surface itself, however, requires a total velocity gain approaching 10,000 feet per second for descent and landing, to which must be added an equivalent amount for takeoff. Any round trip to the lunar surface thus imposes a requirement for nearly 20,000 feet per second over and above what is required to reach lunar space in the first place. This fact has important practical implications which will be discussed later.

Since the moon has essentially no atmosphere or magnetic field, both it and the lunar space around it are as subject to solar flare radiation as is far-orbit space. The remarks made about far-orbit space in this connection thus apply to lunar space as well, except that the moon itself undoubtedly provides some shielding in its shadow out to distances which depend on the degree to which solor-flare particles travel either in straight lines or act as a plasma.

Beyond the major gravitational influence of the earth lies interplanetary space, where solar gravity predominates throughout, except for local planetary effects. Thus it is no longer meaningful to speak of earth orbits, although terrestrial gravity can produce significant perturbations in solar orbits millions of miles away. The vastness of interplanetary space can be conveyed by the fact that, even within the orbit of Mars, the circular wedge-shaped portion extending outward from the sun, including ten degrees on either side of the earth's orbital plane, contains over two million billion billion cubic miles, nearly 20 thousand billion times the volume of near-orbit space and 27 million times that of far-orbit space. Even within the inner solar system, interplanetary regions comprising the sun, Mercury, Venus, the earth, and Mars are so extensive that travel across them can take months or years.

OCEANS FOR FUTURE NAVIES

The nature and characteristics of the space arena, as outlined above, suggest a number of potential inherent benefits and limitations of military operations in the various regions.

First the proximity to earth targets of near-orbit space is vital to certain reconnaissance and surveillance operations, especially those involving high-resolution optics which become impractically complex and cumbersome at distances greater than a few hundred miles. Nearness also has the advantage that transit energy and time requirements are relatively low for vehicles operating within this region, and traveling between it and the earth.

Aside from these benefits, however, near-orbit space is an awkward operating region for a number of reasons. For manned operations especially, it is a hazardous and undersized arena by nuclear standards, as pointed out previously, especially in view of the fact that only one or two nuclear bursts, properly sized and located, might render it inaccessible to man quickly and for long periods by increasing the intensity of the trapped radiation belts. Nearness brings with it ease of detection and tracking of satellite vehicles, which can perform evasive maneuvers only with great difficulty and which are subject to anti-satellite ground fire by interceptor rockets which could be small, simple and inexpensive compared to the vehicles required to place target payloads of significant size and weight in orbit in the first place.

In addition, nearness to earth carries the disadvantage of very limited earth coverage, both with regard to line-of-sight for reconnaissance and communication satellites, and target coverage for antisurface or antimissile weapons in orbit. In either case, this limitation demands large numbers of satellites in orbits of widely varying inclinations, and this in turn imposes cost and complexity penalties which tend to wash out or overbalance the cost advantages of remaining close to the earth. Limited maneuverability in near-orbit space also imposes, under many circumstances, long waiting times before an orbital vehicle can be returned to a preselected landing site, which is a constraint potentially incompatible with the classical military requirements for flexibility and quick response.

The Van Allen Belt even in its natural, let alone augmented, state, makes the inner part of the magnetosphere an inhospitable region for sustained operations. It is possible that special reasons may develop for placing in the proton belt a heavily shielded manned station, or less heavily shielded unmanned satellites for detection, monitoring or relay, but it seems probable that this will be the exception rather than the rule, because of the hazards associated with such operations, and the high costs of lifting the shielding into orbit.

The magnetosphere must be traversed to enter far-orbit space, so that it could function either as a gateway or an obstacle to the regions of space beyond. If an antagonist so chooses, he may maintain the Van Allen Belt in an augmented state by a time-phased series of nuclear bursts, forcing his adversary to enter space through the polar openings at latitudes greater than 45 degrees. This would impose propulsion penalties either for maneuvering to increase orbit inclination or for northward or southward launches where the advantage of the earth's rotation is lost, unless the launch site is located at latitudes of 45 degrees or greater.

In this connection, it is interesting to note that the three major Soviet launch sites are so located, Tyuratam at 45.6 degrees, Kapustin Yar at 48.5 degrees, and Plesetsk at 62.7 degrees. In contrast, the two primary United States sites are well underneath the Van Allen Belt, Cape Kennedy at 28.5 degrees, from which range safety limits prohibit very northward or southward launches, and Point Arguello at 34.6 degrees.

This could create an incentive for the Soviets to go to deep space for extended operations, since from their high-latitude launch sites they cannot, without heavy maneuvering penalties, launch into near orbits which are free from near-polar segments unprotected by the Van Allen Belt, from solar flares, or from overflight of U.S.

territory. The United States, however, can avoid Soviet overflight by merely launching approximately eastward from Cape Kennedy. Such constraints as are imposed by fixed launch sites could give rise to strong incentives for both the United States and the Soviet Union to develop some kind of airborne mobile launch platform to permit space launches to be made essentially from any desired point, in any desired direction, at any desired time.

In the outer regions of the magnetosphere, where Van Allen Belt electron fluxes are much less intense, lie the synchronous altitudes, where orbital periods are close or equal to that of the daily rotation period of the earth. Here, satellites in circular equatorial orbits may be made to "hang" stationary over a fixed point on the equator, or describe daily figure-eight traces about it, if inclined or elliptical orbits are used. Expanded line-of-sight coverage and ease of keeping track of satellites in these fixed or localized positions, render synchronous orbits very useful for communication relay, meteorological, and navigation purposes as well as other geophysical and space experiments. Low radiation levels would permit manned operations, although for military missions the advantages of synchronous deployment could be overbalanced by vulnerability because of possible ease of detection and surveillance resulting from deployments which are relatively localized.

It is difficult to see clear military advantages of operating on the moon itself, because of the heavy propulsion penalties imposed by each landing and takeoff. The mass of the moon may provide effective solar flare and nuclear shielding, if lunar operations are established beneath the lunar surface. Yet for propulsion penalties much less than the 20,000 feet per second accumulating with each lunar landing and takeoff, more than adequate amounts of

57

shielding can be placed in far-orbit space, and furthermore at a location of one's own choosing rather than being confined to the moon which would be an easily located and uncomfortably small arena in any nuclear exchange. In fact, the total surface area of the moon is under 15 million square miles, less than 26 per cent of the land area of the earth, or only slightly greater in area than the Sino-Soviet territory, or Africa; and on the moon, there are never any clouds under which to hide. As with the Van Allen Belt, it is conceivable that some special military requirement might call for accepting the expense and hazard of a military lunar operation, but such would seem to be the exception rather than the rule.

A stronger possibility would seem to be the eventual extraction of rocket propellants from lunar materials, which can be shown to promise potential significant economic advantages for high energy operations such as far-orbit or interplanetary missions. If used in support of military systems, however, such lunar propellant plants would be subject to the above limitations of vulnerability. If lunar propellant plants did prove feasible and were established, studies indicate that the most economical method of operation would be to carry the propellants by special tankers into lunar or far orbit, where actual refueling operations would occur, rather than conducting these operations on the lunar surface.

Far-orbit and interplanetary space, which are here combined under the term deep space, appears to offer a number of potential military advantages, arising primarily from its vast size, by virtue of which it includes the weaker portions of the magnetic and gravitational fields. It is free of magnetically trapped radiation although subject to passage of solar-flare particles, it offers possibilities for increased vehicle maneuvering, it increases line-of-sight and target coverage of the earth, and within its tremendous volume it offers the possibility of hiding space vehicles, much as airborne alert aircraft used to be able to lose themselves in the skies, or naval forces on the seas, and as submarines may still be hidden within the oceans. Interception of far-orbit vehicles cannot be accomplished with relatively small and inexpensive rockets, but would require interceptor systems approaching in cost and sophistication the targets themselves. This is true whether the interceptors are launched from earth or from stations in space because in the latter case, the system must include all that is required to deploy and maintain the interceptor in space in the first place.

The analogy can be drawn between space and the oceans as military arenas, and though imperfect as with all analogies, it is instructive. If the earth's surface and atmosphere are imagined to be the shore and the surf washing upon it, then near-orbit space is like a narrow sound, bounded on its outer reaches by the magnetosphere, a hazardous reef of trapped radiation and steeply rising gravitational potential. This reef is passable in its natural state, but parts of it can be mined, forcing the enemy to search for special channels to gain access to the high seas of far-orbit space. Once upon those vast stretches, vessels are very difficult to locate unless continuously tracked and even then may escape through evasive maneuvers, and cruise undetected and battle-ready for weeks or months. The moon is like an island costly and difficult to land upon, and perhaps too small and too easily pinpointed as a base for strategic operations, but which may offer yet undiscovered potential.

The high seas are too vast for anyone to control continuously in their entirety, or at least they were in the early days, so the custom has arisen for military forces of

59

opposing nations to operate upon them with relative freedom of movement. The same situation may develop in deep space. But near-orbit space, inside the reef of the magnetosphere, is all within easy range of small, relatively simple surface-based interceptors. It therefore appears quite feasible for any nation to achieve and maintain control of the near-orbit regions above its own territory on earth, much as states in the past and present have controlled the seas immediately off their shores with coastal batteries. Large and costly military space systems may therefore not be appropriate to near-orbit space, just as major naval vessels do not normally operate within range of enemy shore batteries, except perhaps for special dash missions.

Precedents for this may have been established by the capture of the U.S. intelligence ship, *Pueblo*, operating near the coast of North Korea in 1968, and more particularly the downing of a U-2 reconnaissance plane from an altitude of about fifteen miles by Soviet ground rockets in 1960. Although that was an airborne rather than an orbital vehicle, it would be superficial to merely assume that an undesirable manned or unmanned spacecraft at, say, 100 nautical miles altitude would not also be attacked, especially since this would not involve an interceptor of much greater size, complexity or cost.

It is true that most space activity to date has been in near orbits, including many undesignated flights by both U.S. vehicles and the Soviet Union's Cosmos series, which are widely regarded to be of a reconnaissance nature. This would have been predictable on the basis of two fundamental factors, that access to near-orbit space is technically easier than to deep space, and that near orbits are required for high-resolution optical reconnaissance. These aspects may have established the beginnings of precedent

60

for all orbital space (i.e., above 50 to 100 nautical miles altitude) to be regarded as open to free international access, as are the high seas. Legal studies have resulted in similar recommendations for a ceiling on national sovereignty.

The relative ease, however, of negating near-orbit vehicles by ground fire must force this question to remain open, until it is determined just how a space power will react if and when it is actually subjected to overflight in near orbit by a potentially hostile vehicle which it regards as provocative and which it can intercept. It is a matter of record that for more than five years the United States Air Force has had in readiness at Johnson Island in the Pacific, a pilot antisatellite system designed around the Thor missile, and the press have reported that the Army has conducted experiments at Kwajalein with antisatellite adaptations of the Nike-Zeus and Nike-X antiballistic missiles. It would seem reasonable to assume that the Soviets also possess or are developing anti-satellite capabilities. How would we react to the disabling or capture of one of our military satellites by the Soviets? The existence of such capabilities, combined with the relative ease of intercept and the U-2 and *Pueblo* precedents, inject at least considerable uncertainty into the future of near-orbit jurisdiction and military operations.

In space, new kinds of relationships may develop between opposing forces. There may be many situations where by reason of great distance, camouflage or inability to approach closely, the identity or purpose of a potentially threatening object cannot be determined, in which case some probabilistic doctrine may be invoked, indicating that an attack upon it is warranted. Actually, that kind of decision may have to be faced before long if, for example under some circumstance we are confronted with

61

an unidentified satellite where we are truly uncertain whether its mission is peaceful, or whether it is an orbital weapon (fractional or otherwise, single or MIRV). If these possibilities turn out to be realistic, then sporadic hostilities in space could evolve into a kind of ongoing cold war of attrition. Such encounters, however, might be very unlikely to propagate back and result in destruction on earth.

A useful way to characterize the space arena is in terms of vehicle velocity required to gain access to various portions of the arena. Delivery and logistics systems constitute a major portion of the cost and effort of operation in any distant arena, and development of flexible and economical transportation systems capable of meeting the high power requirements is a major technological key to establishing an operational capability in space. It is therefore important to acquire some grasp of the vehicular performance requirements for access to the space arena.

These requirements can be conveniently represented in terms of velocity gain. A transportation mission of central importance to a wide variety of space operations is the round trip from earth to orbit and return, for purposes of crew rotation and resupply, and the cumulative vehicle velocity required for this mission serves as an effective measure of the difficulty of gaining access to various regions of space. Any vehicle capable of 45,000 feet per second velocity can gain round-trip access not only to orbits up to 50,000 nautical miles altitude, but to all far-orbit space and neighboring interplanetary space as well. Operations in elliptic orbits can reduce this requirement by as much as 5,000 feet per second.

Thus, there is a gravitational "reef" as well as a magnetic one, and the propulsive capacity to climb over this reef is a primary benchmark for space transportation performance, since it opens up essentially all the vast operating regions beyond. This gravitational-magnetic reef is thus a kind of fundamental threshold of the space arena, inside of which are the potentially hostile near-earth regions within easy reach of ground fire, and beyond which stretch the sanctuaries of deep space.

SURPRISE, SURVIVABILITY AND STRATEGY IN SPACE

A central aspect of cold war strategic competition between deterrent and potentially aggressive powers is the critical need for the deterrent side to maintain survivability of its strategic weapons, against surprise attack by the other side. The potential aggressor, for his part, strives to tip the balance of power in his favor through constant efforts to devise new and improved methods for achieving surprise.

In this competition, technology and time currently seem to favor the potential attacker, by providing increasingly effective systems with global reach, which are gradually eroding the survivability of earthbound deterrent forces. Near-orbital bombardment systems threaten to be able to catch the majority of bomber forces on the ground with surprise attacks, multiple warheads increase the vulnerablity of land-based missiles to massive accurate strikes, and satellite and underwater detection methods are invading the high-seas sanctuaries of surface ships and submarines.

As deterrent systems become increasingly vulnerable they tend to lose their credibility and value as retaliatory capabilities. Surprise attack looms more effectively against them, thus rendering them useful only for surprise attack. As a result, the stability of deterrence weakens and the probabilities of war can only mount.

63

In these circumstances, the above described characteristics of deep space and the implications of strategic operations there offer what may be the only realistic promise not only of maintaining but of greatly enhancing the survivability of strategic systems, and thus protecting the stability of deterrence. For deep-space deployment promises unprecedented potential for survivable strategic operations such as retaliatory bombardment and command control stations. Paradoxically, it also promises new opportunities for surprise. These statements are of primary significance, and the reasons underlying them warrant consideration in some detail.

Consider a deterrent system deployed in space. Attacks against it, from earth or from positions in space, can be attempted either by volume weapons such as large nuclear bombs, by more selective weapons such as smaller nuclear bombs or nonnuclear warheads carried by guided rockets, or by very selective weapons such as focused radiation beams.

The effectiveness of volume weapons depends on the relative scales of the weapon destructive capability, and of the arena or volume in which it is employed. Since nuclear destructive radii are substantial compared to the scale of the earth and near-orbit space, nuclear weapons promise to be quite effective volume weapons in these arenas, and sustained or extensive manned operations there may be very hazardous. Here, the attacker need not know the precise location of his targets, and employment of defensive decoys as a defense would mean only that the decoys themselves would be destroyed along with the targets. Only a limited number of nuclear warheads of current size, if burst in near-orbit space, could envelop a large portion of that arena and of the earth's surface. In deep space, however, the situation

64

is reversed, and "mining" of this arena for volume coverage would involve hopelessly large totals of nuclear warhead weight. Here, the problem of volume destruction is overwhelmingly difficult, even in the event that warhead efficiency could be increased to that achievable by the total annihilation of matter.

The attacker therefore must resort to selective rather than volume weapons, against deep-space systems. What are his prospects? Regardless of the type of weapon he uses, the attacker must in this case not only be aware the target exists, but also must know its location with reasonable precision.

Against near-orbit targets, as a basis for comparison, the attacker's prospects would be good because he could detect and track them accurately, they could not maneuver much because of their high orbital velocity, and he might achieve an effective initial antisatellite capability with modified versions of present single-stage ballistic missiles, and ballistic missile interceptors such as the Spartan missile of the Safeguard system. The weakest element in such a capability probably would be the ground-based warning radars, which might be large and relatively soft (i.e., vulnerable). They could be hardened to some degree by being reduced in size or placed underground. If they were still vulnerable, then the attacker could always fall back on volume instead of selective destruction against near-orbit satellites.

The formidable task, however, of detecting and tracking objects in deep space, let alone negating them, appears to lie far beyond foreseeable radar, optical and infrared technologies. Why? Because three different capabilities must be achieved and exercised at the same time: first, the ability to detect electromagnetic emissions or reflections from objects so far away; second, the ability to pick up and locate such signals through indiscriminate searching of sector upon sector of space; and third, the establishment of adequate numbers of search and detection facilities in space, to cover the tremendous volumes in which strategic systems could hide.

With regard to detection, even for very advanced radars, the basic radar equation shows that skin-tracking, a one-square-meter target 10,000 to 50,000 miles away, requires transmitted power at each installation in the order of tens of millions of kilowatts, or ten to twenty times the power output of Grand Coulee Dam; and since detection range varies merely as the fourth root of both power and target cross-section, it is quite apparent that radar detection at hundreds of thousands or millions of miles, will long lie beyond practicality. Optical detection at up to 20,000 miles has been mentioned for Baker-Nunn cameras sensing reflected sunlight against a known star background, but even this capability could be defeated readily if the target were made a mirror-like reflector beaming reflected sunlight away from, rather than toward the camera. Infrared appears even more hopeless than radar and optical detection, partly because of the difficulty of sorting out a weak or distant target source against the ever-present background of natural radiations from the cosmos.

Even when detection at a certain range is technically feasible, if the existence or exact location of an object is uncertain, then there will be the further practical problem of directing the radar, optical or infrared sensor in sweeping patterns to cover all of the sectors of space in which the presence of the object is suspected, until a signal is obtained. This can be a long, frustrating procedure, as shown by the experience of the laser reflector experiment of the Apollo 11 (first man-on-the-moon) mission. In that case, a device specially designed to reflect laser beams was set up on the lunar surface, and laser beams were shot at it from the Lick Observatory in California and the McDonald Observatory in Texas. Even knowing with close accuracy just where Apollo 11 landed in the Sea of Tranquility, it took the Lick telescope twelve days of searching, and the McDonald telescope thirty days, to pick up a reflected signal. This was using a target whose presence and location were known, and which was designed to be reflective. In the light of this example, the far greater difficulty of picking up a distant target whose location and even existence are uncertain, and which is designed to be non-reflective should be obvious.

When the problems of detection and searching are eventually solved, and if reliable surveillance can be achieved by in-space search and detection facilities out to radii of tens of thousands of miles or more in all directions, then the truly overwhelming problems of establishing enough such facilities to cover the staggering volumes in question must be faced. For example, if a single facility can maintain surveillance of a sphere, say 100,000 miles in diameter, then to cover all space within a million miles of the earth, *thousands* of such facilities (each with a power output of several Grand Coulee Dams) would be required; and as pointed out previously, there is no definite limit on the distances to which strategic space systems can be deployed—they can be sent out millions of miles. Clearly, there is more than enough space in which to hide.

The difficulties faced by all the above approaches could be compounded even further by use of target shaping, orientation or coatings to reduce telltale radiations in the direction of a would-be attacker's sensors, as well as by the use of sham radiation sources to confuse him, and random maneuvering.

67

Alternative ways of locating the target include intercepting communicatons from it, and trailing it or its supply flights from launch, with a "shadow" vehicle. Communications interception could be overcome by "spoofing" or other electronic countermeasures, or by communicating through relay satellites, many of which could also be hidden in the depths of space at random locations, or by communicating via highly directional laser beams if this proves feasible. The shadow may be confused and defeated at some point or points along the flight path by releasing decoys, large numbers of which can be carried at acceptable weight penalties.

The chances of detecting, locating and tracking distant systems in space thus appear slim at best with foreseeable technology. Even if this problem were overcome, the problems of actually making the attack are comparably formidable. Each shot would require a large multistage launch vehicle. Though the attacker has the advantage of being able to approach the target from a variety of angles and velocities of his own choice, the target can complicate his problem by maneuvering, jamming radar and other sensors, deploying decoys and launching active defense of some sort.

The attacker might try to overcome such defenses by attacking in salvo, but at this point the attacker's cost picture begins to compound even further. The use of focused radiation beams might increase the attacker's effectiveness, particularly against maneuvering and decoys, but only if the attacker has first located his target, and only if such beam weapons can eventually be powered, focused and aimed adequately to be effective across great distances. Further, if the attacker possesses such devices, so in all likelihood will the defender, who may use them to increase the effectiveness of his defense.

68

In addition to all the above difficulties, if the attack against the space force were made from the earth, the attacker would have to launch his missiles and thus tip his hand hours or days ahead of time, since such periods would be required for earth-launched missiles to reach their targets in deep space.

Deep-space systems will require supply operations originating on earth and passing through near-orbit and magnetosphere space, and because of reduced survivability in these regions such operations are potentially a weak link. It was pointed out previously that since it appears feasible to control all near-orbit space above any given territory on the earth's surface, near-orbit operations involving orbits passing over that area may be subject to de facto prohibition as soon as truly effective surface-to-space antisatellite capability is developed, and an occasion arises which instigates its deployment and use. On the other hand, it seems just as improbable that any nation would attempt, or be permitted, to control near-orbit space above another country's coastal waters or airspace, which means that supply flights to deep space could pass through near-orbit space safely, provided they do not overfly hostile territory. Even if the enemy augmented the Van Allen Belt with nuclear bursts, using perhaps the justification of "scientific experimentation" or weapon "testing," it would still be possible to reach deep space by traversing the magnetosphere through the Van Allen Belt "holes" above the polar regions.

Accomplishing this without overflying enemy territory places a premium either on launch sites far from the equator, or mobile launch platforms. Such flexibility of launch and recovery operations would be a primary objective of any program to develop military space capability. It would be absolutely required in a hot war environment anyway, since in that case no fixed launch site on earth would be inviolate to enemy action. However, even if the supply lines to manned stations were cut for some periods of time, the station crew duty cycle must be long enough—if the system is to be economically viable at all (see Chapter III)—for station operations to continue uninterrupted for several months without a supply flight, or before the crew would exhaust their provisions and have to return to earth. This length of time should be sufficient to include most nuclear exchange scenarios. Given adequate flexibility of earth-based launch and support operations, and adequate crew-stay times, it seems very likely that military systems in deep space can be highly survivable for a long time.

These considerations of survivability carry different implications for different kinds of military missions. It is not implied, for example, that for reasons of survivability all military missions would be conducted in deep space.

As previously noted, certain kinds of policing missions, such as earth reconnaissance and surveillance, must be conducted close to the earth because of inherent limitations in sensor equipment, particularly where precision photo-reconnaissance is involved. Also, inspection of potentially hostile satellites must be conducted wherever those satellites are located, and if they are in near-orbit or magnetosphere space, then that is where the inspector must operate. Some of these policing missions may be accomplished unmanned, in which case the question of vulnerability may be less important than the question of whether conduct of such a mission will be regarded as provocative, or otherwise politically undesirable. Others may require the benefits of man's unique capabilities, in which case the consequent risk to human life must be treated as in any hazardous military operation. Whether the risk is taken will depend on how great it is, and on the criticalness of the situation.

In certain cold war circumstances, manned reconnaissance or inspection flight over enemy territory, though subject to antiaircraft or antisatellite operations, may be tolerable to both sides, with no danger of increased hostility or violence. They may even be accepted as a stabilizing influence where either side is seeking evidence or confirmation of the other's intent. The Cuban missile crisis of 1962 can be cited as an example.

In a hot war environment, it is probable that manned near-orbit reconnaissance and inspection flights would be extremely hazardous missions, but there may be cases where the risk would be justifiable and volunteers forthcoming as has generally been the case in the past. With regard to surveillance missions extending over longer periods of time, certain functions may be accomplished by unmanned satellites, but surveillance operations so complex as to require continuous manned maintenance and operation, seem of questionable military value in near-orbit or magnetosphere space. Such a system would require a considerable investment in manned stations and ground support activity, and commitment in human life, which must certainly be written off immediately at the outbreak of a hot war, and which would thus be of no use for trans- and post-attack information gathering.

In addition to enhanced survivability, deployment of bombardment systems in deep space promises, also, unparalleled opportunities for surprise. A primary reason for this lies in the aspect of survivability mentioned above, that it may be possible by deployment at extreme distances, cross section control, decoys, and random maneuvering, to render such systems essentially undetectable or untrackable. Nothing contributes more to surprise than

71

covertness of operation. One of the main reasons why surprise was virtually complete in the attack on Pearl Harbor was that the Americans were unaware not only of the whereabouts but even the existence of the Japanese carrier task force which launched the attack.

Deep-space bombardment stations would have the inherent advantage, since they are in effect firing "downhill," of being able to reach any target on earth or in space with relatively small missiles which can be designed for very short, perhaps almost impulsive, burning times. Because they could be small, many could be controlled from a single station, and they might be launched undetected even though the bombardment station may be under distant radar surveillance. Because their burning times are short, it seems likely they could be fired without being detectable by infrared sensors, especially if they are deployed at such distances from the controlling station such that any infrared surveillance would be forced to operate in a continuous searching or sweeping mode.

The warheads could be sent on their way toward the targets in any of a variety of trajectories of the attacker's choosing, so that either earthbound or space targets could be attacked from many directions and at many velocities. Use could be made of some variant of the so-called space bus of the MIRV system, which is a guided maneuverable carrier which can accurately release several warheads toward their separate targets, allowing them the economy of utilizing a common guidance and propulsion system. Earth targets could be approached at all angles and at literally meteoric velocities of at least 36,000 feet per second, compared to ICBM approaches which are by and large constrained to a narrow attack tube and to maximum speeds of about 23,000 feet per second.

The defenders' problem of detection and warning

72

under such circumstances, especially if he is attacked in salvo and if warhead penetration aids such as decoys and cross-section control are employed, appears formidable if not hopeless within foreseeable technology. The first warning an earth target may receive of an attack from deep space could be reentry streaks in the sky only seconds before the targets are struck.

At this point will be noted the frequently discussed concept of another kind of orbital surprise attack system, namely, that consisting of one or more nuclear bombs of very large yield (such as in the order of 1,000 megatons or more, sometimes referred to as "gigaton bombs"), in near orbits which pass over enemy territory. Such bombs could cause widespread damage to populations and agricultural crops through thermal flash and resulting firestorm effects, could be detonated in orbit or in the fringes of the atmosphere on command from the ground, thereby achieving essentially zero delivery and warning time and, in a sense, absolute surprise against earthbound soft targets. In addition, the fallout effects from such space bursts might be small even though the bursts occurred near the atmosphere, so that such devices would not quite approach the absurdity of the "doomsday machine" mentioned previously.

Since they would be effective only against soft targets, however, they would not appear useful as counterforce instruments but rather as propaganda or terror weapons by a desperate or reckless aggressor. They might be of some use to him as an aid in bargaining, especially if there existed no satellite inspection capability to ascertain whether his orbital bombs were real or sham. His psychological gains, however, would be countered at least in part by the picture of desperation and irresponsibility thus presented to the world, and by the extreme provocativeness of the system. These considerations are aside from the near-orbit vulnerability difficulties of such a system, even if unmanned. Everything considered, the desirability of near-orbit gigaton bombs for either deterrence or attack appears doubtful.

Strategic bombardment and command control capabilities in deep space, however, are natural goals for both deterrent and aggressive powers. For deterrence these capabilities promise survivability which is indispensable in the bargaining period which could precede and follow any initial exchange of blows, and for aggression they promise the new opportunities for surprise described above.

The fact that weapon delivery times from deep-space deployment areas may be days, weeks or even months, would not seriously mar the effectiveness of such systems. If used as a second strike capability for deterrence, the delivery time is of secondary importance anyway, provided the system is survivable and can penetrate enemy defenses. If in special cases coordinated strikes with short warning times are required, the weapons can be dispatched toward their targets at appropriate intervals for simultaneous arrival. If the strike is to be recalled, the weapons could be destroyed or diverted, if necessary, just before reaching the targets or coming within range of enemy detection and warning perimeters. This would be not unlike airborne recallable strike missions, where in times of crisis strategic bombers can be dispatched toward enemy borders and, upon arriving there, may be either recalled or permitted to continue to the targets as the occasion may require. If used as a surprise attack capability, a deep space bombardment system may reduce warning times to seconds or minutes, as pointed out previously, essentially regardless of total delivery time from launch to impact.

The fact that with deep space systems such great distances are involved would be of itself no problem to the effectiveness of command control and communications systems deployed there. A command post in deep space, because its functions are executed by electromagnetic transmissions at the speed of light, would be no more than seconds removed from the forces it controls, a few minutes at most even if it were located millions of miles away, even on or in the vicinity of another planet or one of its satellites.

The promise of enhanced surprise from space against earthbound military targets can be counted upon to be strong bait to a potential aggressor seeking a way to alter the deterrent balance. If he gets there first with an effective strike capability, he will have obtained a formidable bargaining instrument. It should be noted, however, that it is primarily against earth targets only that such surprise can be achieved initially, because just as a bombardment system itself can be hidden in deep space it is likely that other strategic systems which are its potential targets can be, as well. This situation can be changed only by the eventual development of detection, identification and tracking methods beyond the limits of immediately foreseeable technology.

For this reason, the strategic sanctuary of deep space should provide powerful cause for a deterrent power, also, to begin to move in that direction as the survivability of its earth-based deterrence erodes.

Enhanced survivability and surprise aside, strategic space systems have other potentially attractive characteristics. One such feature, for example, would be the availability of still another mode of weaponry to be added to existing—land, sea, air—deterrent forces. Consequently, before he could risk attack with any confidence of success, a would-be attacker would be required to cope with a complex of coordination problems. Also, if military satellites systems deployed in space were by chance detected on occasion, sporadic attacks upon them could be accepted as a "fact of life" in outer space. Although the resultant strategic competition might involve continuing cold war hostilities in deep space, it would seem most unlikely to ignite destructive activity on earth. Indeed, thereby, international tensions could be reduced and international stability strengthened.

It is not suggested that deep space strategic systems would be any more effective in deterring limited war than earthbound nuclear systems have been. To the degree, however, that space systems could increase the stability of deterrence and thus ease global tensions, they could lead to an improved general environment in which the use of force at any level would be less likely than in the past.

This discussion of war and space has so far been essentially general, without much specific reference to the actually developing U.S.-Soviet strategic competition. How has the cold war begun to extend to space, how might it lead to the evolution of deep-space strategic systems, and what kinds of challenges does this present to the United States? Consideration of these questions requires first an appraisal of the nature and feasibility of strategic space systems, to gain some grasp of the engineering and economic problems which must be overcome in their development.

III

STRATEGIC SYSTEMS
IN DEEP SPACE

Give me where to stand, and I will move the earth.
ARCHIMEDES

We have spoken of the promise of strategic systems hidden in deep space. What would such systems consist of? How soon might they be feasible from an engineering standpoint? What major technological problems would have to be solved? How much would such systems cost to develop and operate? Who might be able to afford them, and when? We will consider these questions at some length, to picture what may be feasible directions for extending the strategic arms competition to space, and to obtain a grasp of the scope and scale of a systems engineering and management challenge which could have fundamental impact on traditions and institutions within the United States.

Strategic systems in deep space would include, first and foremost, some means of delivering force against strategic targets, either on the earth or in space. A deterrent power would want to hide these forces so that they could not be destroyed by an aggressor, and could serve as a retaliatory threat. A potential attacker would strive for such hidden systems to enhance his own capability to launch a surprise attack "out of nowhere." Thus, either case implies the capability for bombardment from orbit. That is not the whole story, however, for these bombardment systems would be useless without the necessary means for communicating with them and maintaining command and control over their operation. Command and communication facilities require transmitting and receiving antennas and other equipment that is relatively fragile and difficult to protect against nuclear attack. As earthbound hiding places for such installations are exhausted or eliminated, and as techniques are further perfected to black out earthbound radio communications by electrical disturbances from nuclear bursts in the upper atmosphere, it seems reasonable to expect that motivation will grow stronger to locate these systems, also, in deep space.

In addition to force delivery and command control, strategic space operations would inevitably include reconnaissance, defensive and various supporting functions as well, which are discussed in more detail later.

The character of all these elements, however, will depend essentially on which of the many possible design approaches are ultimately selected for the bombardment and command systems themselves. This in turn depends, perhaps most strongly on a single basic question: should the system be manned or unmanned, and if man has a role to play, what is it?

The following discussion will begin, then, by considering man's capabilities and limitations as an element in strategic space systems.

MAN AND THE ECONOMICS OF SPACE OPERATIONS

Two kinds of reasons may exist for man's presence in a space operation. First, he may be absolutely required as a direct participant in executing whatever mission is to be accomplished. Second, if the direct performance of the mission is automated, man's presence may be advantageous for practical or economic reasons because of his abilities to service, maintain and repair the mission equipment.

A strategic command post in space happens to be an excellent example of a system in which man can be considered an absolute necessity. The command post is nothing more than a protective shell with communications equipment to sustain and serve the commander and his staff. To replace the commander with a computer would be to relinquish command to the computer. This is not at present generally thought to be desirable and in any case will not be technically feasible for some time, even granting rapid advances in computer technology. Thus, it seems clear that this system would consist of some kind of space station (or stations) deployed in deep-space orbits, which would contain life support equipment for its command staff and station engineering personnel, maintenance facilities, perhaps some means of changing its orbit and defending itself, and of course all of the necessary communications, electronic and computer gear to support the command and control functions. The staffs and crews would be rotated, and the station resupplied, by periodic logistic flights from the earth.

Absolute requirements for man's presence in space also may be said to exist in the case of space bombardment systems, though for different kinds of reasons than with the command post. Where missiles are stationed in space, it is obviously of critical importance to provide some highly dependable means of assuring that the weapons are always in an adequate state of readiness, to protect them and their supporting equipment from spying and sabotage, and to prevent accidents resulting, for example, from equipment malfunctions which could cause unintentional deorbit and attack.

It is conceivable that functions such as these could be performed by computer-operated robots, but who would be willing to entrust so completely critical responsibilities for national and world security to machines? Probably very few. Certainly man's natural capacities are limited, and he requires the aid of various equipments in space to augment his own capabilities. For example, various sensing instruments can exceed the range and sensitivity of man's sight, hearing, smell and touch, and computers can go far beyond his capacity, speed and accuracy in performing complex calculations. Yet there is little prospect that ma-

81

chines will soon be able to compete with or exceed man's ability to recognize old patterns in new settings, his tolerance of temporary work overloads, and his capacity to "change his program" and adapt to new and unforeseen situations. Nor is it probable that machines will soon appear—within reasonable weight, reliability and cost limits—which could simulate man's muscular and skeletal flexibility and dexterity. No foreseeable machines can approach human judgment, which renders man unequaled in his ability to integrate, discriminate and process large quantities of various kinds of information and make decisions rapidly against a wide range of uncertain and changing alternatives.

It therefore seems reasonable to expect that a strategic bombardment system in deep space would consist of one or more manned stations, each serving as a maintenance, control and firing center for a number of missiles. Each missile would consist of a nuclear warhead (or perhaps a multiple warhead), a guidance package, and a propulsion unit. Since the system would be located beyond the strongest regions of the earth's gravitational field, the warheads would require only short propulsive bursts to send them on their way toward their targets, and so could be much smaller than the earthbound ballistic missiles such as Titan and Minuteman, to which we have become accustomed. In fact hundreds of deep-space missiles might be controlled from a single station. They could be located either within the station itself (as Poseidon missiles are carried within their nuclear submarines), or stored immediately adjacent, or deployed in some manner within a few miles (or hundreds or thousands of miles) of the station, in which case they could be serviced and maintained by space tenders ranging out from the station as a base. The crews would be rotated and the station supplied at intervals by shuttles from earth.

For similar reasons, the presence of man undoubtedly can be very helpful in certain missions, such as reconnaissance and satellite inspection, where his ability to make pilot observations, to decide when and where to photograph, to make fine adjustments in precision equipment, and to process and interpret new data on the spot, could be invaluable. He has demonstrated in the Gemini and Apollo flight programs his capabilities for performing critical functions in the inspection of foreign objects in orbit, such as manually controlled rendezvous including chasing maneuvers where necessary, extravehicular inspection, disassembly and negation, and adapting to unforseen situations and emergencies. To the degree, however, that these missions must be performed in near orbits, especially overflying hostile territory, where ground fire would be a significant threat, and in proximity to foreign objects which could be readily and effectively booby-trapped, such missions probably would be of short duration, and undertaken as hazardous actions only when special requirements dictated. They may be compared in this respect to dash missions such as commando operations or reconnaissance aircraft flights along hostile shorelines and airspaces.

Man's vulnerability in space, particularly at great distances from nuclear bursts, has already been noted in Chapter I. This could place strict limits on the use of manned systems for certain kinds of military missions, especially, as just mentioned, those which must be performed in near orbits. However, if deep-space systems such as the command post and strategic bombardment force in question are to be effective in the first place, they must be well enough hidden to reduce the chances of their being subject to direct attack. Thus, for these systems, man's vulnerability to nuclear bursts would be a far less critical issue. Actually, such stations would need shielded "storm cellars" aboard in any case, to protect the crews for days at a time during the passage of high-energy radiation particles from flares or storms on the sun, which occur at sporadic intervals. This necessary shielding would provide a degree of protection against nuclear attacks as well. The shielding weights involved could be fairly large without greatly impairing the economics of the deep-space station concept, because this weight would have to be launched into orbit only once and its associated costs can then be spread over as long a time period as desired, since its depreciation rate in space should be negligible.

Man's unique and diversified capabilities have already begun to be demonstrated convincingly, in both the United States and Soviet manned space flight programs, and it seems clear that he will be an essential element in any really complex operations in space as well as on earth. There is no real substitute for him yet nor can technology promise a comparably sophisticated and dependable robot for at least several decades. Yet the blanket argument is still often heard, that the inclusion of man in space systems does not make economic sense because of the added weight and cost of equipment needed to protect and sustain him in the space environment, and that this weight would better be allocated to additional unmanned equipment. This is an oversimplification, as even a brief look will show.

The weights needed to provide for space crews depend on the number of men in the crew and the length of time they are to stay in space. For example, if allowance is made not only for the crew and their spacesuits, but also their food, water, gases, environmental control, power supply and cabin structure, the total weights involved for a sixty-day mission probably would be about a ton and a half for one man, six or seven tons for five men, and ten to twelve tons for ten men. In other terms, this works out less than fifty pounds per man-day as the weight penalty for manning a space operation. There are, of course, many missions which can be performed adequately by small satellites weighing only tens or hundreds of pounds, and in these cases the penalties imposed by manning would be excessive. For space command and bombardment systems, however, which would involve total weights in space of up to hundreds of tons, the few tons required for manning would be little enough to pay for man's inimitable capabilities. There is an old saw among technologists: "Where aside from man, can you find a durable, adaptive, non-linear machine with over ten billion electronic elements, which is comparatively cheap, weighs only 150 pounds, and can be mass produced by unskilled labor?" The answer is nowhere yet, and probably not for a long time.

We return now to the second possible reason mentioned at the beginning of this section, for man's presence in a space operation. That is, his ability, proven clearly in the Gemini and Apollo flight programs, to service, maintain and repair equipment in space. Consider that the astronaut is a maintenance and repair man only, and ignore for the time being his other possible contributions. Then a fairly straightforward comparison can be made of the costs of operating the system both with manned maintenance and without. At least three basic modes of system operation are conceivable: total replacement, earth-based maintenance, and station-based maintenance.

In the total replacement approach, when failure of an element or elements of an unmanned payload impairs overall performance below an acceptable level, the entire payload is replaced through an unmanned launch. To save the cost of procuring and launching an entire payload, it might be attempted to replace only that element or module which failed, but the practical and engineering

85

problems involved seem to make this an unlikely way of going about it. A variation on the total replacement mode is to return the failed payload to earth, where it is repaired and then relaunched. This saves the cost of a new payload, but this saving would be more than balanced by the added costs of deorbit and recovery systems.

Earth-based maintenance would involve launching a manned utility vehicle which performs rendezvous with one or more malfunctioned payloads, then returns to its base on earth after maintenance and repairs are made in space.

In station-based maintenance, all operations are conducted using as a base not the earth, but a manned space station which is in turn supported logistically from the earth. From the station, entire new payloads can be launched to replace malfunctioned ones, and manned tender vehicles can shuttle to failed payloads, repairing them in orbit or returning them to maintenance shops in the station. By virtue of its location in space, the station itself may be suitable as a deployment point for one or more mission payloads, which would then be directly accessible for maintenance at all times. This would be advantageous, and may be absolutely required for very complex equipment which needs frequent servicing and repairs.

Earth-based logistic flights for these three modes of operation, especially where the systems are deployed in deep space, could be direct from earth or could involve refueling from tankers pre-positioned in near orbit. If improved booster technology eventually permits placing large amounts of propellant in orbit at relatively low cost, then refueling may offer some economic advantages. However, the vulnerability of such near-orbit operations to ground fire and Van Allen Belt augmentation makes them a potential weak link in military operations, so it seems likely that direct flight would be the preferred method for logistic shuttles.

If the costs of these three modes of operation are compared, it can be shown that any of the three may be preferable from a cost standpoint, depending on certain conditions. The circumstances that determine which mode is most economical are, primarily, the weight and cost of the equipment to be maintained in space, the average lifetime of unmanned equipment before it fails, the length of time a crew can man a station before a relief crew is needed, and the costs of booster and shuttle flights. Thus, for example, when mission payloads are relatively small and cheap (as space equipment goes), and can be expected to perform unattended satisfactorily for, say, more than a year or two, then total replacement would be the economical choice in most cases. If, on the other hand, the mission equipment to be maintained is heavier and more costly, manned maintenance of some sort would be economically preferred regardless of mean-time-before-failure. How the man is utilized, whether in trouble-shooting flights "as needed" or in a space station on a continuous basis, depends mainly on the comparison between the mean-time-before-failure of the equipment, and the length of the tour of duty for the station crew. The longer the mean-time-before-failure, the more preferable is earth-based maintenance, and the longer the crew duty cycle, the more preferable is station-based maintenance.

For the strategic command and bombardment systems in question, there can be little doubt that station-based maintenance is the most economical way to proceed, providing crew duty cycles of at least sixty to ninety days can be achieved. Also, the station-based approach carries less technical and economical risk, since if the mission equipment turns out to be less reliable than anticipated (and in practical experience this often is the case), increased numbers of total replacement or earth-based maintenance flights would be required, and the costs of these two modes would soar far above their predicted estimates.

A further indication of primary importance that emerges clearly from such studies is that the economic effectiveness of strategic space systems depends very heavily on booster and shuttle transportation costs as well as on station crew duty cycles. This points to two technological objectives which should receive high priority as goals in the national space program: development of low cost reusable boosters and spacecraft, and extension of manned stay-times in space.

If this kind of cost comparison is applied to other types of space operations than the systems considered here, it becomes readily apparent that many future space systems, and most complex long-duration missions, will require the presence of man, if for no other reason than the economics of maintenance and repair alone.

Experience with unmanned and manned equipment to date seems to bear this out. Of the first forty or so attempted interplanetary probes by the United States and the Soviet Union, there have been only nine flights in which the equipments functioned long enough to reach their planetary destinations and transmit data back successfully: Mariners 2, 4, 5, 6 and 7, and Venera 4, 5, 6 and 7. While these nine were properly hailed as triumphs of exploration and yielded scientific data which surely justifies the many attempts, such lack of dependability could not be tolerated in operational systems. Reliability has been increased significantly in recent years in certain types of unmanned equipment, such as satellites for communication, navigation and weather surveillance, but these de-

88

vices are relatively uncomplicated compared to the strategic systems under discussion here. Many other unmanned and undesignated United States and Soviet satellites have been placed in orbit, often referred to in the press as possible reconnaissance devices, but these have almost always remained in orbit only a few days. In contrast to this experience with unmanned devices, the first seven years of manned space flights appears to have been without failure, until the death of Cosmonaut Vladimir Komarov in the flight of Soyuz 1, in April, 1967. It seems to be common sense that man must be a central element in the exploration and use of space, and the heavy Soviet and American emphasis on development of manned space capability is a concrete reflection of this understanding.

As the necessary components of manned space systems are developed first by the United States and the Soviet Union, and later become available to other nations, it should be possible to constuct and operate a space command post for under one half billion dollars per year, and a space bombardment system for less than five million dollars per warhead annually. Thus a system of, say, three command posts and one thousand warheads controlled from three maintenance and firing stations could be assembled and operated for something in the neighborhood of five billion dollars per year. These figures are based on use of present Saturn V-class launch vehicles for deployment and logistic flights, and could be reduced considerably if low cost shuttles are developed. (They do not include the costs of research, development, and ground facilities, since these can be spread over a number of years and probably can be applied to several programs or missions.)

If there is anything surprising about the costs of

strategic space systems, it is not that they are high, which should be expected from the outset, but that they are not much more than the comparable costs for earthbound systems. For example, the total funds allocated for strategic retaliatory forces in the United States Government Budget for fiscal 1969 was 9.6 billion dollars. In the post-1975 era, when strategic space systems might be anticipated, the U.S. Gross National Product is expected to have grown beyond a trillion dollars and that of the Soviet Union to be approaching the trillion-dollar level. In that period, even if the above estimates are two or three times too low, the cost of such space systems would amount to no more than a fraction of one percent of the GNP of either the United States or the Soviet Union.

It is clear, then, that extension and gradual shifting of the strategic armaments competition away from the earth would present no real economic obstacle to either of the two great space powers. Nor, as the required technologies are developed and begin to disseminate, would it be beyond the capacity of Japan, Germany, the United Kingdom, France, Communist China or any other technically advanced nation within the next few decades.

SHUTTLES, STATIONS AND THE TOOLS OF THE TRADE

Before such strategic space capabilities can be mastered, a kaleidoscopic array of new aerospace equipment and vehicles will have to be produced. These necessary developments will be described briefly to illustrate that, while almost all of them could be undertaken today on the basis of technology already in hand, their scope and diversity would produce an impact throughout the industrial fabric of any nation undertaking such a program.

90

The achievement of strategic space capability would depend on the development of three basic types of military hardware: mission equipment, space vehicles, and support systems.

By mission equipment, we mean those devices which provide the necessary extensions of man's own capabilities for sensing, handling information, and delivering force, so that he can perform what might be called five classical functions: policing, command control and communications, force delivery, defense, and supporting activities.

Policing requires equipment for sensing, reducing, evaluating and storing data, for reconnaissance, surveillance and inspection missions. It also involves devices for limited force delivery and disablement which may be required in conducting inspection and patrol activities. Especially important is the development of sensors which can function effectively over the great distances in space, such as high resolution telescopes and cameras to observe enemy activity (particularly on the earth), infrared sensors to monitor enemy rocket vehicle movements and other heat-producing events, high-power radio and radar equipment to locate and monitor enemy transmitters, and radiation sensors to detect nuclear bursts, power systems and other sources of radiation.

Mission equipment for command control operations must include power sources, transmitters and antennas for generating, sending and receiving communications, data-handling systems for processing and storing information, and equipment for data readout, facsimile and display to facilitate on-station alertness and efficient decision-making. Secrecy must be protected in vital communication links, necessitating special equipment for appropriate programing of the frequency and intervals of transmitting and receiving power, and for encoding and cryptographic work. The promise of greatly enhanced security of space

91

communications is offered by laser techniques, which may provide coherent light beams capable of carrying very large quantities of information which, being highly directionalized, may be almost impossible to intercept as they stab through space.

Force delivery across the space arena, whether against targets on earth or other celestial bodies, or in space, requires two fundamental elements: the force package or weapon itself, and the delivery system.

The five basic classes of weapons are, as given in Chapter I, conventional, nuclear, chemical, biological and radiological. As we saw there, at least the first four are militarily useful against earth targets. Against space targets, however, the utility of the various types of weapons is yet to be evaluated. Because of their great lethal ranges in space and the absence of the undesirable side effects associated with fallout, nuclear weapons appear to have a natural applicability, especially against manned systems. Where highly localized effects are desired, such as in inspection-negation missions, the usefulness of conventional weapons such as rifles, shotguns, shrapnel grenades and orbiting pellet clouds, all of which would benefit from lack of atmospheric drag and wind, is apparent. Determination of the utility of chemical, biological and radiological weapons against targets in space must await further research, testing and experience.

Delivery across the space arena can be achieved presently only by properly guided rocket propulsion, although other propulsion modes such as some form of antigravity or force field interaction, are dreamed of for the distant future. For reasons of storability, readiness and operational reliability, it seems probable that propulsion for weapon delivery in space will be by solid propellant rockets at least initially, particularly since as already pointed out, the launching of weapons from deep-space positions will not require propulsive maneuvers of great energy. Such propulsion schemes are already feasible within the present state of solid rocket technology. A far more serious problem is that of guiding such delivery systems across great distances which have no precedent in earthbound operations. For example, the longest ranges required of earth-to-earth ballistic missiles are limited by the size of the earth itself and do not much exceed 10,000 miles. In contrast, weapon delivery across the space arena, whether space-to-earth, space-to-space, or earth-to-space may involve launch-to-target distances hundreds or thousands of times greater. Such problems of guidance technology probably can be overcome through improvements in techniques for inertial, stellar, and perhaps map-matching guidance, as well as the use of fine corrective maneuvers along the trajectory. It is, nevertheless, a problem requiring intensive effort, and which must be solved in any case to render feasible a wide variety of both military and nonmilitary activities in the space arena.

The more distant possibility of radiation beam weapons is in a class by itself, since no meaningful distinction can be drawn between the weapon and the delivery system. As mentioned in Chapter I, extensive technological improvements must be achieved in the areas of beam focusing and compact power sources, before these devices become practical.

Defense of military or nonmilitary resources and operating systems, whether earthbound or in space, against enemy policing, command, and force delivery, can be either active or passive.

Active defense can include interception, in which case the above comments about weapons and delivery systems apply here also, or electronic countermeasures. In either case, the capability to detect, locate, track and monitor enemy vehicles and installations is critical. Accomplishing this across great distances in space will be a foremost and difficult objective for military space technology.

Passive defense can include use of camouflage, decoys, hiding, shielding and the interposing of distance by deployment, dispersal or maneuvering. The space environment may offer numerous opportunities for utilizing variations of these basic techniques. For example, in space, camouflage may mean the use of paints or coatings which do not reflect optical or radar signals, or which duplicate the thermal background of the space environment itself. Decoys may be used which, because of their deployment distance and lack of such familiar outside forces as gravitation, wind and weather, may be quite effective though constructed relatively lightly and cheaply. The possibilities of hiding in space are much more promising than on earth, because of the unlimited distances which are available and the relatively infinitesimal size of space vehicles and systems, which can be made to appear even smaller by proper shaping to control their apparent cross section to radar beams and other sensing devices. The use of shielding in space, against both natural (solar flare) and weapon radiations, as well as against conventional (pellets or shrapnel), chemical or biological weapons, may be attractive in some cases since, as noted previously, shielding of any desired thickness can be built up over a period of time, it must be launched only once, and its depreciation or degradation in the space environment should be negligible.

In addition to the equipment required for the above four classes of missions, specialized devices would be needed for various supporting operations. For example, docking, sealing and transfer mechanisms are required for logistic, resupply and refueling activities, and specialized tools, design of equipment for maintainability, as well as extravehicular suits and maneuvering devices would be priority items for efficient servicing and repair in space. Mechanical as well as electronic and chemical equipment will be necessary for medical and rescue operations, specialized sensors and transmitters for weather surveillance and navigation, and a wide variety of instrumentation for test and exploration activities in the space environment. Of special interest is the design of equipment for conducting biological and chemical testing under zero gravity, especially where such testing involves the handling of fluids. Work in this area might result, for example, in entirely new forms of medical treatment and chemical processes.

So much for a brief scan of the kinds of mission equipments which would be necessary. From the little that has been said, it should be obvious that the description of such requirements could progress endlessly into much greater detail, and would range across the entire horizon of computers, electronics, nuclear engineering, power generation, industrial chemistry, biomedicine and many other fields.

Of more immediate priority than mission equipment, however, is the question of what kinds of aerospace vehicles will be needed, for it is impossible to do anything in space without launch vehicles, spacecraft, space stations and other transportation devices for placing men and materials in space and for enabling operations to proceed there, in orbit, on the moon, and eventually other planets. For this discussion, we may think in terms of three classes of vehicles: earth-based, space-based, and satellite- or planet-based.

Earth-based vehicles are those designed for the job

95

of transporting various payloads from the earth to space and, where necessary, back again. Thus, there are two types: one-way vehicles, which we shall call either "small" boosters (if their payloads are less than, say, fifteen tons) or "large" boosters for larger payloads, as well as round-trip vehicles which we shall call, "shuttles."

The United States, the Soviet Union, a European combine, France and Japan have all developed or are developing families of small boosters. In the United States they are Thor, Atlas, Titan III and Saturn IB in combination with various upper stages such as Delta, Agena, Centaur and Burner II. The Titan, Saturn and Soviet Proton boosters are the largest, each capable of placing nearly fifteen tons in near orbit. The European Europa, the French Diamond and Emerald, and the Japanese Lambda series are presently limited to payloads under one ton. Large boosters are under development in both the United States and the Soviet Union, in the form of Saturn V with a payload capacity of 140 tons in near orbit and nearly 50 tons in deep space, and a somewhat larger Soviet vehicle. Even thousand-ton capacity boosters have been studied at least in the United States under The Nova and Orion projects, but it seems likely that boosters already in existence, perhaps in modified and improved versions, will continue to do yeoman service for the world's space powers for years to come. Saturn V-class boosters for example, would be adequate for placing in deep space any of the strategic systems considered here.

Typical booster payloads would include active hardware such as mission equipment and life support systems, passive hardware such as structures and radiation shielding, and expendables such as propellants. For some missions, including interplanetary expeditions requiring large amounts of propellants, the boosters might be converted to serve purely as tankers.

96

By contrast, typical shuttle payloads would include station crews and other space operations personnel traveling between the earth and their tours of duty in space, as well as certain priority items of mission equipment, spares, supplies and life support fluids which might be needed with urgency or at frequent intervals. Shuttle payloads would probably fall in the range of ten to twenty tons.

Because of the required frequencies of these flights, shuttle vehicles must be operationally flexible, and because such flights represent the major recurring and accumulating cost element in almost all continuous manned operations, they must be economical in terms of dollars per pound transported. By definition, at least the manned portions of these vehicles must be recoverable, and considerations of both operational frequency and economy strongly suggest that the remaining vehicle hardware should be mostly, if not totally, recoverable and reuseable, and capable of rapid and economical refurbishment and turnaround. The fact that shuttle payloads are relatively small, and that consequently the associated vehicles can be also, appears to favor flexibility, recovery and reuse. This is not to say that development problems associated with such vehicles are minor. They are great, but certainly within the limits of foreseeable technology. The Americans and the Soviets have already developed the first crude ancestors of such vehicles in the Mercury, Gemini, Apollo, Vostok, Voskhod and Soyuz projects. The United States had pursued development of a more advanced shuttle vehicle in the form of the Dyna-Soar orbital glider until that program was canceled in 1963. Development of the truly advanced descendants of these shuttle vehicles is perhaps the most critical key to the opening of space for extensive exploration and use. More will be said about this later on.

The next class of vehicles, which we call space-based,

97

include manned space stations having little or no maneuvering capability and maneuvering orbit-to-orbit vehicles.

The primary function of manned space stations is to provide a habitable base of operations for manned space activities. To reduce the cost and complexity of crew rotation and resupply operations it is critically important that space stations provide adequate environmental control, internal living and operational volumes, radiation protection and gravity simulation as needed, in order that the crew duty cycle can be extended as long as possible. The Soviet Union is already well underway in developing a manned space station, as evidenced by link-up of the two, two-man Soyuz 4 and Soyuz 5 spacecraft on January 16, 1969, creating in effect a four-man station. Each spacecraft included a work-rest module which can be left in orbit. In this way a large space station can be built up over a period of time, and this can be expected before long. The United States is developing a manned space station to develop such techniques in its three-man Orbital Workshop program, which is scheduled for first flight in 1972. Space stations are in many ways attractive as operational bases. Since they probably will not have to be recoverable, except perhaps in special cases, and since they are free of gravitational forces, space stations can be expanded to almost any size and shape desired, with the possible qualification that they may be required to simulate gravity by rotation. The vacuum environment should result in a practically negligible depreciation rate, aside possibly from low-order meteoric erosion and occasional puncture, so that the high cost of manufacturing and deploying a space station—including the necessary large amounts of radiation shielding—can be amortized over long periods and perhaps over a number of different missions.

To realize their full potential, space stations probably will require smaller adjunctive maneuvering vehicles, manned or unmanned, which would be called "tenders" or "tugs." These devices would be designed for use in space only, and would play supporting roles in servicing, repair, construction and experimental activities.

It has been suggested that manned orbit-to-orbit maneuvering vehicles may be necessary for certain space missions requiring maneuvering velocity gains beyond the capability of vehicles whose propulsive efficiency is compromised by design provisions for reentry and recovery. Velocity capabilities up to 30,000 feet per second or more will be required to attain extensive space maneuvering flexibility. The only practical design concept which could meet such velocity requirements within foreseeable technology is that of a single-stage-non-reenterable vehicle using a nuclear rocket such as has been successfully developed in the U.S. Nerva program. Even using nuclear propulsion, however, the weights of propellant required for each refueling cycle appear to be in the range of several hundred thousand pounds per tankful, and since the cost of this propellant in orbit must include not only its manufacture cost but the cost of launching it as well, it would appear that such vehicles would be used sparingly and only on critical missions. Further, it appears questionable whether important military operations would be allowed to depend on the refueling and refurbishment of such non-reenterable maneuvering vehicles in near-orbit space, because of the previously emphasized problems of vulnerability in that region, both to enemy ground fire and to augmentation of the Van Allen Belt. For this reason, as well as the reduced maneuver-velocity requirements in deep space, it seems likely that these operations would be found militarily practical only in space regions

99

beyond the magnetosphere. Furthermore, while deep-space vehicles may be subject to solar-flare shielding weight penalties, these penalties are smaller than the propulsion weight penalties imposed on near-orbit-based vehicles by the requirement to escape from, reinject into and maneuver in, low orbits.

Such vehicles may be rendered practical by the development of advanced propulsion techniques offering much higher performance levels, such as electrical, nuclear gas core, and nuclear pulse propulsion. It appears, however, that electrical propulsion will not yield sufficiently high thrust to meet the probable military requirements for quick reaction, high accelerations and short mission times. The technical feasibility of gas core, and nuclear pulse propulsion (studied under Project Orion), has yet to be demonstrated on other than a theoretical basis.

The conduct of operations on the moon, other planets or their satellites, will require the development of a third class of vehicles, capable of landing on, taking off from, and operating on the bodies in question. If the body has no atmosphere, the vehicle must be designed for approach and landing by controlled propulsive maneuvering and must have shock absorption equipment to permit the vehicle to survive final contact in operable condition. Such capability has been demonstrated by the Surveyor soft lunar touchdowns, and developed further in the Apollo Lunar Module (LM). If the body in question has an atmosphere, then the thermal shield, configuration, propulsion and landing mechanisms must be designed and integrated so as to operate throughout the necessary atmospheric and velocity regimes, utilizing the atmosphere to best advantage wherever possible. When such a vehicle is eventually required, the technological problems involved will be similar to those associated with earth-space-earth shuttle vehicles. Operations on the planets and their satellites eventually will require, in addition to landing and take-off vehicles, specialized devices to operate on and beneath the surfaces of the widely varying compositions, consistencies and structures of the various planets and their satellites. Development of these vehicles doubtless will be based on the technologies of earthbound land and amphibious vehicles and their modifications.

Operations in the space arena will require various kinds of ground-based supporting systems, located on the earth, the moon or other bodies. These include launch and recovery bases, detection-tracking-communication networks, and refurbishment and checkout facilities. While it may seem natural to dismiss such systems as being of only secondary importance to the design and conduct of space operations, this would be a critical misjudgment, particularly where military systems are concerned, for at least two reasons.

First, ground facilities often contribute a major portion of total systems and operations cost, and ground systems design can be a primary factor in the overall economic optimization of the system. That is, it may in some cases be economically desirable to accept more complex or costly alternatives in flight hardware design, if by reductions in ground system costs this can result in a more economical total system.

Second, and perhaps more important, because they are located on earth, which has already been shown to be a confined arena in which fixed installations of known location are especially vulnerable, ground systems can be weak links in space operations. For example, if military space operations depended on elaborate launch installations like those at Cape Kennedy or Vandenberg Air Force Base, those operations could be easily curtailed either by

101

destruction of the launch facilities, or by augmentation of the Van Allen Belt, if these facilities were located beneath the belt. The transmitters and antennas required for detection, tracking and communication installations, may constitute large, soft targets, and their basic survivability potential is inherently low. It goes without saying that destruction of these installations might cripple military operations in space, by impairing the command and logistic structure upon which they must be based. Such considerations emphasize the importance of reducing the number, complexity, and vulnerability of ground-based facilities.

The major problems of earth-based support systems appear to be problems of design and operational concept rather than of technology, which is already generally well developed. For planet- or satellite-based support systems, however, where surface or subsurface structures must be constructed and operated in extraterrestrial environments, the technology problems may be similar in part to those associated with manned space stations. Indeed they may be more difficult in the sense that provision must be made for unfamiliar gravitational, weather, surface and subsurface conditions, about which knowledge is still in its infancy.

In addition to development of the mission equipments, vehicles and support systems themselves, the operating techniques and general know-how for utilizing these systems must also be evolved, including, checkout and launch, abort and rescue, rendezvous, maintenance and repair, establishment of crew duty schedules, simulated gravity, refueling, reentry, landing and recovery, refurbishment and turnaround, and so on. Most of these operating phases will require some degree of manned control and participation. Development and training associated with such methodology can improve greatly the reliability and general effectiveness of these operations. Since the learning and application of this know-how must be based on practical experience and ingenuity, however, and cannot be derived entirely by paper planning, mistakes, accidents and improvements on the practical level must be expected before they are utilized with routine efficiency.

THREE KEY BUILDING BLOCKS

From the above survey of hardware systems and operating techniques, all of which will be eventually required for military, and indeed for most nonmilitary operations in space as well, it is obvious that the necessary technological developments are practically boundless in scope and magnitude. The effort required to develop all of these space capabilities would absorb the combined technological resources of the whole industrial world for a long time. Thus, these tasks cannot be attempted all at once, but they don't have to be and shouldn't be, since it can be expected that the requirements for various operations in space will not appear simultaneously, but will evolve in sequence. For example, it is surely reasonable to expect that requirements will develop for orbital before lunar operations, and that lunar operations will be required before activity on other planets or their satellites. Because of this, it is possible to identify three basic capability developments which are of primary initial importance and which can be regarded as critical keys necessary to open the door to routine operations in the space arena. They are: the development of an advanced manned shuttle vehicle, the achievement of extended duty cycles for crew operations in space, and the development of improved navigation and guidance systems to direct vehicles accurately across dis-

103

tances measured in hundreds of thousands or millions of miles.

A central requirement for the future exploration and use of space, is the development of a reusable shuttle vehicle which can transport men and equipment from the earth to space and back again, on an economical and routine basis. It has already been emphasized that the physical presence of man will be necessary, especially in military operations where on-the-spot judgment and maximum dependability are vital, and that there are strong reasons for expecting manned military space systems to be deployed beyond the magnetosphere, in far-orbit or interplanetary regions. Shuttle vehicles are critically important, because they are the one element instrinsically required for any manned activity, and because the cost of their operation is cumulative with time and can become the dominating economic factor in manned space systems, eventually eclipsing even the research and development costs themselves. This is not to say that such shuttle vehicles can alone confer all the necessary capabilities for military operations beyond the earth. Other kinds of systems, such as outlined above, must be developed as well. Important as they may be, however, the manned shuttle vehicle is inevitably the keystone to military space capability as a logistic, rescue and special mission vehicle. As such, it is worth some discussion.

The performance objectives of the earth-space-earth shuttle vehicle system arise from two basic requirements: operational flexibility and economic effectiveness. It is proposed that operational flexibility requires four basic capabilities of the shuttle vehicle system. First, its payload must include adequate numbers of crew and passengers, and sufficient cargo weight for mission equipment and resupply. It has already been noted that a payload between ten and twenty tons should cover these items. Second, its velocity must be sufficient to allow round trips to deep space which, as stated in Chapter II, require at least 40,000 to 45,000 feet per second. Such velocity potential lends the vehicle another kind of flexibility as well, since for near-orbit missions it can be translated into both increased payload capacity and orbital maneuvering capability. Third, it must provide the functions of rendezvous, docking and transfer of men and materials. Fourth, it must be capable of mission durations associated with the round-trip shuttle flights to deep space, which range up to perhaps twenty days but probably not much longer. It appears, therefore, that these shuttle missions will be shorter than the periods for which solor-flare prediction techniques can assure safe travel reliably, so that the shuttle can avoid the weight penalties of solar-flare shielding.

Economic effectiveness requires at least three additional important characteristics of the vehicle. First, since most of the cost of manufacturing and operating such vehicles is associated directly or indirectly with the manufactured hardware cost, it is desirable to reduce this quantity. Second, for the same reason, it appears desirable to reuse most or all of the vehicle as many times as possible, provided that the vehicle can meet the third requirement of economical and rapid refurbishment. It must be recognized, however, that if refurbishment cost is a large fraction of the original cost, and is a lengthy process, in the long run it may be preferable both operationally and economically to purchase a new vehicle for each flight.

In addition, there are three capability objectives involved with both questions of operational flexibility and economic effectiveness. First, it seems likely that routine, low cost vehicle recovery and turnaround can be best achieved through the capability for aircraft-type landing at a preselected site. The reasons for this are associated with the fact that parachute recovery, which is the other primary alternative, requires relatively large recovery areas, can involve severe landing impacts and damage especially under gusty wind conditions, and requires some means of transporting the recovered vehicle from possible inhospitable terrain to the refurbishment area, whereas a tangentially landable vehicle can to a large extent perform this function itself. Second, the vehicle must have aerodynamic maneuvering capability to reduce the waiting time required for return to a preselected site from orbit, and to be used as an aid in near-orbital maneuvering by dipping into the fringes of the atmosphere. It is important to note that vehicle configurations which can accomplish horizontal landing tend to provide aerodynamic maneuverability as well, so that these two requirements go hand in hand. Third, it is naturally desirable to minimize the number of vehicle stages required and to avoid in-space refueling, since staging and refueling both tend to decrease reliability, and because during a refueling operation system survivability may be seriously reduced.

There are many different ways in which these capabilities could be combined into the shuttle vehicle system, but even brief consideration can throw some light on what may well develop to be a few of its primary characteristics. The payload, velocity and no-refueling constraints, for example, essentially determine that, within the bounds of foreseeable propulsion technology, the vehicle must have at least two and perhaps three stages.

The first, or lift-off, stage probably will employ chemical rather than nuclear propulsion at least while still within the atmosphere, because of the problems of hazard, engine maintenance and weight penalties from radiation shielding, required by large nuclear engines. It may employ rocket propulsion with vertical take-off, or air-breathing propulsion (perhaps combined with rockets) with horizontal take-off, the requirement for maximum recovery and operating flexibility perhaps favoring the horizontal take-off mode. This, of course, would also carry with it the horizontal landing capability. Its structure, to operate effectively through a wide spectrum of velocities in the atmosphere, may involve variable geometry such as the swing-wing of the F-111 supersonic military aircraft. Since in most optimization analysis of vehicle performance, the first-stage velocity remains within ranges associated with aerodynamic flight, it is natural to think of the first stage as essentially an airborne platform which could serve as a mobile launch site for space vehicles, or as a large airplane for earthbound missions. If in this manner, sufficient launch flexibility could be achieved to permit deep-space launches from points and at times of one's own choosing over wide areas of the earth, then the mobile airborne launch platform concept could be a critical factor in reducing the vulnerability of launch operations, which have already been mentioned in this and the previous chapter as a potential weak link in military space operations.

The middle stage, if there is one, would burn out at such a velocity that it might make a looping trajectory through the most hazardous portions of the Van Allen Belt, and in any case, would reenter the atmosphere far away from the launch location. For these reasons it may be unmanned and perhaps expendable.

The final stage is the manned space operating vehicle and must therefore by definition be at least partially recoverable. It may employ chemical or nuclear propulsion, or it may be essentially nonpropulsive except for provi-

107

sions for attitude control and rendezvous maneuvering. It must contain the cabin and life support provisions for the appropriate mission duration, and must be capable of reentry and atmospheric braking upon return from deep space (at reentry velocities of at least 35,000 feet per second), with the capability for aerodynamic maneuvering and horizontal landing. It appears that the configuration would likely be one of the so-called lifting body types, thick but flattened shapes which in conjunction perhaps with variable geometry wing surfaces allow adequate internal volume for the shuttle payload, yet are able to provide aerodynamic lift and control characteristics for atmospheric maneuvers and horizontal landing.

Selection of the earth-space-earth shuttle vehicle design will require frequent decisions arising from the fact that in most cases those design characteristics which tend to lower cost tend also to degrade performance, and vice versa. It is therefore worthwhile to consider this fundamental question: which is more important, operating performance and flexibility, or low cost? It seems probable that economic studies of various vehicle design approaches will not identify one particular concept as greatly superior economically to all others, but will disclose instead several different concepts which are economically competitive, and that final selection will therefore be made on the basis of performance, flexibility and available technology. For example, vehicle concepts would not be acceptable which require costly and vulnerable launch-and-recovery facilities and operations, which have marginal payload and velocity capability, which have less than near-perfect reliability, and which require weeks or months for refurbishment and checkout. Indeed it will, in practice, be worth a considerably more costly system to achieve less vulnerable and more efficient launch-and-recovery operations, increased performance margins and dependability. In the present and future eras, when the earth has become an undersized arena and hence a most hostile environment in time of war, survivability, quick reaction and dependability will be critical requirements.

A second key to regular space operations is the extension of crew duty cycles. Since man will be a critical element of future space operations, and since the logistic costs of transporting him and his supplies will be a dominating economic factor, it is very important to reduce the required frequency of these logistic flights by achieving the longest possible tours of duty in the space environment. The extending of crew duty cycles to sixty days or more can yield significant reductions of system operating costs. The most essential step in the direction of this objective is the development of manned orbital space stations for both test and operational purposes. A key question with regard to the extension of crew duty cycles is whether and to what degree a simulated gravity environment is necessary for human survival and performance over long periods. Only a manned orbital station can provide this answer, since a zero- or reduced-gravity environment cannot be simulated on earth for more than a few minutes. In addition, only a manned space station can provide adequate living and operating volume, which should probably be at least 150 cubic feet per man, together with proper atmospheric control to permit satisfactory physiological and psychological performance for extended time periods. For example, the Soviet Soyuz station module accommodates two cosmonauts with a total of about 300 cubic feet of internal volume.

If simulated gravity is found to be necessary, whether continuous, variable or intermittent, total or partial, it can be provided by any of several centrifugal techniques, such as rotating the station by cable or a relatively rigid boom about either a counterweight or another portion of itself, rotating the entire station about itself, or perhaps utilizing an internal centrifuge for intermittent crew conditioning. Although such measures are available, it would clearly be preferable, for reasons of simplicity, reliability and cost, to avoid simulated gravity if at all feasible.

Perhaps this could be accomplished through use of drugs. In space, a combination of effects unprecedented on earth either in kind or degree, such as weightlessness, confinement, isolation and certain types of sensory deprivation may result in such bizarre effects as hallucinations, euphoria, depression and other kinds of disorientation. Use of tranquilizers or other drugs may be useful in controlling such psycho-physiological reactions to permit satisfactory performance over long time periods. On the other hand, it may be found that the environment of space creates conditions like, for example, reduction in fatigue and sleep requirement, under which man's performance may be enhanced to levels not possible on the earth. Drugs may therefore be used to intensify these conditions. Drugs may also be able to increase the body's tolerance of radiation. The Soviets are reported to be stressing studies of this possibility. It is conceivable that such investigations may uncover basically new knowledge and understanding of the human organism.

The third key to regular space operations is the development of improved navigation and guidance techniques, to direct vehicles and delivery systems accurately to their targets across the vast reaches of the space arena. In the first decade of the space age, guidance technology made dramatic progress. For example, several Surveyor spacecraft, after traveling more than 200,000 miles, have

110

landed within five miles of their targets on the moon. This represents an error well within one ten-thousandth of the distance traveled. Translated to an earthbound scale, this would indicate an error of less than one mile for a trajectory of ten thousand, approximately halfway around the earth, which seems consistent with what has been implied publicly about the accuracy of earth-to-earth ballistic missiles. Such accuracies may be adequate for earthbound applications, but the extension of routine operations into the much larger arena of space requires that these errors be further reduced. To maintain an accuracy of one mile in an arena where the distances traveled are increased from, say, ten thousand, to hundreds of thousands or millions of miles, requires error reductions of a factor of ten, a hundred, or more beyond what has yet been achieved.

This can be accomplished within present technology for cases where the target is cooperative, for example, if it provides a beacon which allows the vehicle to perform homing or terminal maneuvers. A typical case would be the routine rendezvous flights of shuttle vehicles. For passive or uncooperative targets, however, such as would confront a weapon in flight, either the beacon must be in effect replaced by development of self-contained techniques for terminal maneuvers, or the accuracy of the basic guidance system must be improved by one or more orders of magnitude. In either case, accuracies can be increased significantly by mid-course propulsive maneuvering such as has been demonstrated in lunar and planetary probe flights.

Also, the development of improved guidance reference techniques—e.g., advanced inertial platforms, star trackers, and gravity-sensing methods—not only may provide increased accuracy by frequent updating, but also, since these systems are self-contained, can enhance the

111

military security of the system. In all cases, the reduction of both weight and cost are central objectives, particularly for guidance equipment on board weapon delivery vehicles, since in such cases recovery and reuse is almost always ruled out by definition, and since space-based delivery vehicles are likely to be relatively small compared to earth-based missiles, because of the low deorbit and maneuvering velocities required.

PROBLEMS, BREAKTHROUGHS AND PAYBACKS

The technological base necessary to build the mission equipments, vehicles and support systems which will be the critical elements of strategic space systems is already nearly fully established. Indeed, achievement of the above three key capabilities to regular space operations depends almost entirely on straightforward engineering development efforts, and not on any technological breakthroughs. Certain critical areas of technology can be identified, however, where significant improvements are necessary, and in pursuit of these improvements, it is conceivable that breakthroughs could occur. In fact, it would be surprising, if they did not.

With regard to the manned shuttle vehicle, progress must be made in the understanding of reentry physics and control dynamics at superorbital reentry velocities up to and exceeding 36,000 feet per second, and in improving materials for both radiative and mass transfer shields against the extreme heating environments of reentry, as well as lightweight insulated structures for space handling and storage of extremely low temperature propellants such as hydrogen. The most critical technical area, however, for the earth-space-earth shuttle vehicle is propulsion. Since this vehicle must operate both in the atmosphere and in space, it may require air-breathing as well as rocket propulsion systems. Here, advanced concepts such as the supersonic-combustion ramjet ("Scramjet") may be household words as they become available on a practical basis in the late 1970's or early 1980's. Because of the severe weight penalties associated with rocket maneuvering in space, it is crucially important to develop high efficiency as well as high-thrust propulsion techniques. In this regard, the gas core nuclear rocket is potentially attractive, and if shown to be feasible within practical weight and volume limitations, development of this propulsion method would be a major technological breakthrough. In this concept, the rocket exhaust is heated by a gaseous nuclear reaction to temperatures which would melt the solid core materials typical in the nuclear rockets being developed today. If this is accomplished in the next twenty years or so, as early research seems to indicate, the result would be nuclear-propelled space vehicles which could literally fly circles around anything which would be possible now.

Even without such advances, however, development of an adequate vehicle could be undertaken immediately on the basis of the existing technologies of lightweight structures, and chemical and nuclear rocket propulsion. A flexible manned shuttle probably could be in operation before 1980, at a cost of less than ten billion dollars for engineering development and testing. There remains only one critical step which must be taken before it can become a reality: the decision to pay this "price of admission."

No such obstacles stand in the way of the other two key building blocks. With regard to the extension of crew duty cycles in space, the critical problems appear to be

113

definition of the requirement if any, for simulated gravity, and detailed determination of man's capabilities and limitations in performing a variety of functions in space. The experimental space stations needed to test these problems are already well into development by both the United States and the Soviet Union, in the Orbital Workshop and Soyuz programs. These stations are expected to be operational in the early 1970's and should be capable of quickly answering the weightlessness question, as well as offering the promise of new knowledge in many other areas. With regard to the development of improved navigation and guidance techniques, as noted above, many aspects of the problem can be solved within existing technology by means of terminal guidance and homing maneuvers, and those aspects which cannot be thus solved may depend most heavily on the simplification and microminiaturization of electronic components, an area of technology which is progressing rapidly and promises to continue to do so. There can be little doubt that improved guidance and navigation methods will be achieved as required.

This is also true of almost all the other mission, vehicular, and support systems outlined in this chapter. Weapon or force delivery technology deserves special comment, because in this area it is conceivable that technological breakthroughs may produce revolutionary changes in warfare as did nuclear weapons and the ballistic missiles. In history, the most dramatic reorientations of warfare have been caused by two kinds of technological advance: 1) increased destructive yield per pound of weapon; 2) increased delivery system speed resulting in reduced delivery time. Neither of these two processes has been carried to its conceptual limit, and although the methods of accomplishing the next impor-

114

tant technical advance in either case are not clear, enough can be foreseen so that it would be risky to rule out such possibilities. For example, the ultimate conceivable weapon efficiency is that which results from the total annihilation and complete conversion to destructive energy, of the entire mass of the weapon. It is not yet known how this could be accomplished on a practical basis, but total annihilation of elementary particles has been achieved in nuclear laboratories. The ultimate in delivery speed is the velocity of light, which cannot be exceeded according to currently understood physics. It is not yet clear how destructive quantities of energy can be transmitted in a controlled and directed manner at light speed, but developments in the field of lasers hint at the possibility of practical "death ray" weapons sometime in the future.

How achievement of the technologies and capabilities discussed in this chapter in relation to military applications, can be transformed into benefits for other human enterprises is a broad and difficult question, and will not be treated here in detail. A few comments can be made, however. Because of the military requirements for survivability, quick reaction, and dependability, the manned shuttle vehicle discussed above should possess a degree of operating flexibility more than adequate to lead to enhanced nonmilitary capability also, particularly if it involves a first stage which can be utilized as an atmospheric transport as well as a mobile launch platform for space vehicles. The extension of crew duty cycles and development of manned orbital laboratories may provide new knowledge having both military and nonmilitary significance which cannot yet be guessed. The development of military space capability will require, in addition to these two basic kinds of vehicle systems, advances across the entire spectrum of technology, including nuclear science, electronic and computer engineering, high and low temperature materials, fluid handling, medicine and biological research. It would seem almost impossible to conduct a technological effort of such scope without making both theoretical and practical discoveries having potential application in almost every aspect of human activity and daily life.

Past examples of military developments which have had great impact in general life are the jet airplane, the jeep, insecticides, emergency medical drugs and procedures, food preservatives, synthetic heat and corrosion resistant materials, high explosives and nuclear energy. Current instances of space developments which are producing beneficial contributions in other areas have been described in a 1968 study of Stanford Research Institute, entitled *Some Major Impacts of the National Space Program.* This study documents how, in its first decade, the national space program became a positive and powerful economic factor in industrializing several areas of the nation, how its advances in materials and aerodynamic technologies have contributed to the metals and chemical processing industries, power generation and aviation, and how research and development in space medicine is likely to revolutionize techniques and capabilties in the fields of public health, medicine and biology. But it is quite certain that such applications will not occur by themselves, and that the transformation of raw technology into other benefits is and will be a great challenge to imagination, foresight and management talents.

In light of the brief considerations in this chapter, the following statements can safely be made in regard to the questions posed at the beginning: Any complex extended operations in space probably must be manned,

116

especially if they are of a military nature. The mission equipments, vehicles and support systems required for performance of many classical military missions in space can be identified and fall within the capabilities of present or foreseeable technology. The primary keys to the opening of space for such military utilization are the manned shuttle vehicle, the extension of crew duty cycles by development of manned stations, and the improvement of navigation and guidance techniques, all of which can be achieved before 1980 without any major technical breakthroughs. Certain breakthroughs can be imagined, however, particularly in the area of weapons and delivery systems, which could revolutionize warfare and perhaps confer absolute superiority on whatever state first achieves them. Whether this happens or not, the less spectacular but more predictable advances across the broad spectrum of technology required for development of military space capability must inevitably produce discoveries which can be applied beneficially in many areas of human activity. Such application is a challenge to technologists, businessmen, government and the military.

If from these considerations any single step were to emerge as the priority requirement, it would probably be the decision to develop an advanced manned shuttle vehicle. This observation is by no means original. The shuttle vehicle has been the subject of design studies in the United States for nearly twenty years, including the canceled Dyna-Soar program and its forerunners and, previous to that in Germany during World War II, Dr. Eugen Sänger's rocket-bomber concept which was the progenitor of Dyna-Soar. The European aerospace community has in the past few years recognized the central importance of such a vehicle to any future space capability. They have referred to it as an Aerospace Trans-

117

porter, and have attempted at various times to use development of this vehicle as a focus and crystallization point for a pan-European space program. In view, however, of the funding and managerial problems which have plagued earlier European aerospace efforts such as the Anglo-French Concorde supersonic transport, the European Airbus, and the European Launcher Development Organization (ELDO), it appears likely that development of the first such vehicle will be left to the United States or the Soviet Union, either of which is technically and economically capable of mounting such an effort.

The nation which first achieves an operational manned space shuttle will take a long stride forward as a space-faring power. It is a logical next step in the developing picture of the cold war in space, the evolution of which is the subject of the following chapter.

IV

THE COLD WAR IN SPACE

Surprise lies at the foundation of all undertakings.
KARL VON CLAUSEWITZ

The cold war, as reflected in space, is a silent race for the high ground. In space, as on earth, it has many facets. There are its outward manifestations: international cooperation such as treaties banning nuclear testing and the deployment of mass destruction weapons in space; provisions for the rescue and return of astronauts, and agreements for the exchange of scientific and weather data. There are the strivings of both sides to reap the utmost propaganda value from each new achievement in the exploration and use of space, in the continuing struggle for world prestige. Less visible than these manifestations, but carrying more fundamental implications for the future, has been the gradual development of systems directly utilizing space for military purposes, particularly by the Soviet Union.

The present discussion will begin by focusing on this latter aspect of the cold war. It is worth special consideration, for it clearly reveals that, in contrast to the official United States policy that space offers little of military value and should be maintained off-limits to strategic systems, the Soviets have placed a high value on the strategic importance of space as a military arena from the beginning of the space era, and have made this an integral part of their strategic planning for the future. Even a brief look at some history will give an insight into Soviet thinking in this regard, and will provide some clues as to the manner in which the strategic arms competition could be expected to extend itself into space.

THE SOVIET INITIATIVE: SPUTNIK, VOSTOK, SCRAG, FOBS AND SOYUZ

The cold war went to space with the surprise launching of Sputnik 1 on October 4, 1957. This historic

121

achievement was utilized with great energy by the Soviet leadership in the months that followed, as a propaganda tool, as the final tangible proof that Russia was no longer a peasant country, and as the occasion for international recognition on an equal basis with the most advanced industrial and technological powers. That this propaganda campaign was an immense success is now history. Not only was Soviet status enhanced in the eyes of the world, but the United States was embarrassed, even to the point of having to reassess its own cultural attitudes toward science and technology, and having to undertake what developed to be a basic reorientation of its educational systems.

To the Soviets, however, Sputnik 1 and its successors were not only propaganda instruments, but in fact the forerunners of strategic bombardment systems in space. Evidence of this was not long in surfacing. While still riding their triumphant post-Sputnik wave of prestige, the Soviets sent out the call for a global summit conference on nuclear weapons development and the arms race in general, in the form of a series of letters from Premier Nikolai Bulganin to the leaders of major world powers, on January 9, 1958. President Eisenhower's answer to this letter on January 12, contained some specific suggestions of his own, most dramatic of which was his proposal for agreements that space be used for peaceful purposes only. It was the Soviet answer to this proposal, on March 15, 1958, which gave the first clue about underlying official Soviet attitudes toward the strategic potential of space and its relation to the cold war on earth. This Soviet proposal on space is of historic significance, since it set the tone for many events which have happened since. It stated, in part:

> It is not some engineering and technical peculiarities of construction that determine the peaceful or

military destination of a rocket, but whether it carries a peaceful sputnik, instruments for the study of the cosmic space, or a nuclear charge in the form of an atomic or hydrogen bomb for the purpose of destruction, and extermination.

One cannot fail to see that in raising the question of banning the use of cosmic space for military purposes, the United States is making an attempt, through a ban on the intercontinental ballistic rocket, to ward off a nuclear retaliatory blow through cosmic space while maintaining its numerous military bases on foreign territories, intended for attacking the Soviet Union and the peaceful states friendly to it with nuclear weapons.

It is necessary to find such a solution of the problem as would insure in equal measure the security of the U.S.A., the Soviet Union and all other states.

This would be served by such a measure as the banning of the use of cosmic space for military purposes with the simultaneous elimination of foreign bases on the territories of other countries, first and foremost on the territories of the countries of Europe, the Middle East and North Africa.

This Soviet position was reemphasized on an official basis at the United Nations General Assembly on November 12, 1958, and again at the Geneva Ten-Nation Disarmament Conference on April 4, 1960, when Soviet delegate Valerian Zorin on both occasions was quite specific in rejecting United States proposals to prohibit bombs in orbit, unless U.S. foreign military bases were removed.

It thus appears the Soviets recognized early in the game that deployment of bombs in orbit where they could be made to approach from any direction, pass 100 or 200 miles above the heads of any country in the world, and from which they could be deorbited for attack on only a few minutes' warning, would to some degree be strategically equivalent to deploying missiles just outside a country's borders, from which an attack could be launched with comparably short warning.

The Soviet concern about being ringed by U.S. bases, and their determination to take action aimed at advancing their position, reached crisis proportions in October, 1962, when the Soviets attempted to establish short-warning intermediate range ballistic missiles (IRBM's) in Cuba. When forced to abandon this adventure, the Soviets probably lost their last chance at extended strategic deployment on the ground, with ocean and space systems being the only recourses left.

By that time, it is clear now, Soviet development work was well underway not only on missile-carrying ships and submarines, but on orbital bombardment capability as well. As early as January, 1960, Premier Nikita Khrushchev had stated in a speech to the Supreme Soviet that he had ". . . in the hatching stage . . . a fantastic weapon."

After successful development of the Sputnik satellites, two major technical problems remained before an orbital bomb could be a possibility: first, the satellite must be made to deorbit and reenter the earth's atmosphere, and second, a large warhead must be developed and tested, since by nature an orbital weapon is less accurate than a ballistic missile and requires a more powerful warhead to assure destruction of its target.

The problem of reentry was solved with the successful recovery of Sputnik 5, a Vostok-class deorbital satellite in August, 1960. This technology was utilized in the historic first manned flights by Yuri Gagarin and German Titov in Vostoks 1 and 2, in April and August of 1961. That the Soviets considered these flights more important than just manned space exploration was indicated in articles by experts which appeared in the Soviet newspapers *Tass* and *Krasnaya Zvezda*, which directly linked the Vostoks with bomb delivery capability. At a reception for Titov in Moscow, Khrushchev stated with his characteristic bluntness, "We placed Gagarin and Titov in space, and we can replace them with bombs which can be diverted to any place on earth."

The solution of the second problem, that of developing a large warhead, was hinted at by Khrushchev at the same reception, when he stated that the Soviets ". . . can build a rocket with an explosive warhead equivalent to 100 million tons of TNT." This was shown not to be an idle boast when, about three weeks later on September 1, 1961, the Soviets broke the voluntary nuclear test moratorium with a high-altitude nuclear test series which included a 58-megaton bomb in the upper atmosphere, on the fringes of near-orbit space.

These two technical milestones having been passed successfully, Khrushchev was finally able to make the following announcement in a major policy address in Moscow on March 15, 1962:

> We can launch missiles not only over the North Pole, but in the opposite direction, too. As the people say, you expect it to come by the front door, and it gets in the window.
>
> Global rockets can fly from the oceans or other directions where warning facilities cannot be installed. Given global rockets, the warning system in general has lost its importance.
>
> Global missiles cannot be spotted in due time to prepare any measures against them. In general, the money spent in the United States to create antimissile systems is simply wasted, as correctly pointed out by

the United States Secretary of Defense McNamara, because they do not justify their purpose. These are not my words, this is what McNamara said.

Seven days later in an article in *Krasnaya Zvezda* titled *"Outer Space and Strategy,"* Lt. Col. V. Larionov stated, "It is recognized in military strategy that outer space weapons will become primarily means for resolving strategic tasks, since their operations cannot be linked with any concrete land, sea or air theater of military operations."

Later that year, a new Soviet book entitled *Military Strategy* appeared, edited by Marshal V. D. Sokolovskii, former Chief of the Soviet General Staff and First Deputy Minister of Defense. This book came to be regarded as the authoritative official statement of Soviet military and strategic policy. It contains the following statements in regard to space:

> However, the Soviet Union cannot disregard the fact that American imperialists subordinate space research to military purposes and that they plan to use space to accomplish their aggressive purpose—a surprise nuclear attack on the Soviet Union and the other socialist countries.
>
> Consequently, the Soviet military strategy acknowledges the need to study the use of space and space vehicles to reinforce the defense of the socialist countries. The need to ensure the security of our Motherland, the interests of the whole socialist commonwealth and the desirability of preserving peace on earth demand this. It would be a mistake to allow the imperialist camp to gain any superiority in this area. The imperialists must be opposed with more effective weapons and methods of using space for

defense. Only in this way can they be forced to refrain from the use of space for a destructive devastating war.

Continued development of Soviet bombardment satellites was indicated in a speech by the Chief of the Soviet Strategic Missile Forces, Marshal Biriuzov, in February, 1963. He said, "It has now become possible, at a command from the earth, to launch rockets from a satellite, and this at any desirable time, at any point in the satellite trajectory."

By September, 1964, Khrushchev was boasting of a "monstrous new terrible weapon," and in the 1965 May Day parade in Moscow, a heavy three-stage missile apparently capable of placing several tons in orbit was unveiled on its mobile transporter. The missile was given the NATO code name Scrag, and although no Soviet claim to the effect was made at the time, there was little doubt that this was their first attempt at an orbital bomb. In July, 1965, the new Communist Party Leader Leonid Brezhnev threatened, "We have enough intercontinental and orbital rockets so that once and for all we can put an end to any aggressors or any group of aggressors." Finally, in November, 1965 when Scrag was shown again at the 48th anniversary of the Bolshevik Revolution, the official newspaper *Tass* confirmed that it was an orbital device, from which ". . . warheads can deliver their surprise blow at their first or any other orbit around the earth."

It is possible that Scrag was a primitive, inefficient weapon. It is also possible that the United Nations negotiations leading to the Space Treaty banning the deployment of weapons in space spurred the Soviets on to develop a second-generation space weapon, which could be deployed on earth but could avail itself of an orbital

127

rather than a ballistic delivery path. In any event, in January, 1967, two days before signing the Treaty, they achieved their first successful test of a new weapon which could be deorbited on its target after making only a partial orbit of the earth, and with but three minutes warning.

On November 3, 1967 Defense Secretary McNamara offically acknowledged the existence of the Soviet orbital bomb, which he referred to as a Fractional Orbital Bombardment System (FOBS), and indicated the Soviets could have the system in operation by mid-1968. Four days later, at the military parade celebrating the 50th anniversary of the Bolshevik Revolution, an advanced three-stage missile designated SS-9 (Scarp), was displayed and referred to by *Tass* as being "for intercontinental or orbital launching."

Two Soviet military officials described this development in revealing terms, as quoted in *The New York Times* for November 17, 1967. The first was Marshal Nikolai Krylov, Commander in Chief of the Soviet Rocket Forces: "Of late the Soviet Union has developed other powerful missiles capable of delivering nuclear warheads to targets along ballistic and orbital trajectories. The warheads of these rockets carry devices to break through the enemy's antimissile defenses."

The second was Colonel General Nikolai Yegorov, chief of the political division of the Strategic Rocket Forces: "At the end of the parade were giant rockets with unlimited range, pinpoint accuracy and flight-trajectory parameters that make nuclear missile blows sudden and unavoidable."

Thus, ten years and one month after the launching of Sputnik 1, through a single-minded and determined development program, the Soviets had achieved orbital bombardment capability and this capability had been recognized before the world, by the United States government.

Less than fourteen months later, the Soviets assembled their first manned space station from the Soyuz 4 and Soyuz 5 spacecraft, and thus appeared well on their way to developing the key technological building blocks for a manned strategic space capability. Such a system could be developed and tested in near-orbit space, and later deployed in deep space as large boosters become available.

Meanwhile, the FOBS development program continued, the most recent flight test at this writing and, it is believed, at least the twelfth in the series, having been launched by an SS-9 from Tyuratam on September 15, 1969 under the label Cosmos 298.

The facts of history show that the Soviets have made no particular secret of their drive toward strategic space weapons. Their early work appears to have been related to attempts to compensate for their relative lack of foreign bases, compared to the United States and its allies. Yet despite the subsequent withdrawal of U.S. strategic reliance on foreign bases, and concentration of that reliance on missile and bomber forces inside the United States, and on Poseidon submarine-launched missiles, the Soviets have pursued orbital bombardment capability with undiminished energy. Why?

The Soviet objective in this pursuit, judging from their own statements, appears to be the reduction of warning times, which is the critical prerequisite to a surprise attack capability. Such capability may be effective initially only against soft targets such as cities and bomber bases, communications and warning systems, because of limited payloads and accuracy, but guidance accuracy does im-

129

prove with advancing technology, and it is probable that the Soviets soon will be able to orbit much larger or multiple warheads. As noted in Chapter III, they are said to be developing a rocket even larger than the U.S. Saturn V, which itself can place nearly 150 tons in near orbit. As these capabilities improve, the Soviets may hope to achieve enhanced surprise against hard targets such as missile silos, and perhaps to force a costly expansion in the U.S. Safeguard antimissile system to try to cope with the multidirectional feature of orbital attack. Because of its unlimited range, FOBS may provide enhanced attack effectiveness against nuclear submarines, if the subs can be located. Perhaps in such ways the Soviets hope eventually to be able to shift the strategic balance in their favor.

That the Soviets desire to alter that balance cannot be questioned, in view of their massive buildup of strategic missiles during the mid- and late 1960's, which points toward their surpassing the United States in total number of missiles before the end of 1970. Because their missiles are large and could each carry multiple warheads, the Soviets could far surpass the United States in total number of deliverable strategic warheads as well. This force, combined with a surprise attack component in the form of FOBS, would constitute a formidable new challenge to the U.S. earthbound deterrent.

In the early 1950's, when the Soviets were faced with an overwhelming strategic bomber force which they could not overtake, they essentially "leap-frogged" the bomber to get a head start in ballistic missiles, and thereby forced into being the strategic missile era. There appear sound reasons to think that in the early 1960's, still faced with an overwhelming U.S. advantage in strategic bomber forces—and now a large U.S. missile force as well—they may have decided to "leap-frog" again to the development of orbital weapons, thereby initiating a new strategic space age.

UNITED STATES REACTIONS

The reaction of the United States to the Soviet Union's extension into space of the cold war, has been characterized by confusion, internal divisions over the military versus civilian roles, reluctance at space-spending in the face of more visible problems on earth, and uncertainty and apprehension about the ultimate strategic meaning of space in world affairs.

There has been an official United States policy, sustained through the Eisenhower, Kennedy and Johnson administrations, that space is for peaceful purposes only, and is off-limits to military operations except for relatively passive functions such as reconnaissance, communication, navigation and weather monitoring. Under this policy, the United States has taken a leading role in promoting the nuclear test ban and space treaties, and has refrained from reacting in kind to the Soviet development of orbital weapons.

Yet uneasiness and criticism of this policy has been given wide and frequent public expression, and despite this policy, military-related space capabilities have continued to develop in the course of the national space program. The history of these events is significant, for they form part of the foundation upon which the future must shape itself.

Some might contend that the initiative in space did not rest entirely with the Soviet Union, since the United States had already announced in 1955, plans to launch a small scientific satellite called Vanguard. Actually, far more significant had been the work of Dr. John von Neumann and Trevor Gardner, then special assistant to the Secretary of the Air Force, leading to their recommendation on February 10, 1954, for a ballistic missile program, which went on to become the initial basis for the United States space effort; and the work of Dr. Walter Dornberger, former German general and chief of the German V-2 ballistic missile project in World War II, who struggled from 1951 to 1957 to gain approval of the Dyna-Soar manned space vehicle project; and of Dr. Werner von Braun, former technical head of Dornberger's V-2 team, who had been denied permission to launch a satellite more than a year before Sputnik 1, and whose army team later did launch the first United States satellite, Explorer I, on January 31, 1958.

But, in the end, Sputnik 1 jolted the world, became the turning point in history, Vanguard and Explorer were too little too late, and what space work had begun to stir in America before October 4, 1957 was all but forgotten in the turmoil that followed. The United States reactions to this and subsequent Soviet initiatives can be viewed in terms of three periods.

The first period lasted from the launching of Sputnik 1 to President Eisenhower's recommendation to Congress on April 2, 1958 for the creation of the National Aeronautics and Space Administration. Of this six-month period, it must be said that the United States was thrown into a state of shock. The public statements of influential leaders ranged from flippancy to complacency, to concern, to near-panic. The mood can perhaps best be conveyed through some of these statements themselves.

Three days after Sputnik 1, a *New York Times* editorial observed, "Rockets capable of performing the satellite feat must be assumed capable of delivering atomic and hydrogen bombs many thousands of miles."

Two days later on October 9, 1957, President Eisenhower held his first press conference after Sputnik:

Question: Do you not think that it has immense significance in surveillance of other countries, and leading to space platforms which could be used for rockets?

Answer: Not at this time. No. I think that within time, given time, satellites will be able to transmit to the earth some kind of information with respect to what they see on the earth or what they find on the earth. But I think that that period is a long ways off when you stop to consider that even now the Russians, who have for many years been working on it, apparently from what they say they have put one small ball in the air.

Question: Are you saying that with the Russian satellite whirling about the world, you are not more concerned nor overly concerned about our national security?

Answer: Now, so far as the satellite is concerned, that does not raise my apprenhensions one iota.

A special assistant to the President for foreign affairs, Clarence Randall, in a speech on October 21, referred to Sputnik 1 as "a silly bauble," "this bubble in the sky," and said he was "gratified" that the Russians had beaten the United States in the first satellite launching. Secretary of Defense Charles Wilson is reported to have said, "Nobody is going to drop anything down on you from a satellite while you are asleep, so don't worry about it." He had already reassured the American public some

133

months before that he "didn't give a damn what was on the other side of the moon."

On November 4, Senator Henry Jackson, Dr. Dornberger and on November 8, Representative James Patterson of the Joint Congressional Committee on Atomic Energy, all voiced their apprehensions about the military and orbital bombardment capabilities which Sputnik 1 implied.

The Democratic Advisory Council issued a policy statement on November 11, which read in part:

> Let us not fail to understand that control of outer space would be a military fact of the highest importance.
>
> The air war of yesterday becomes the space war of tomorrow. We have fallen behind in these weapons of tomorrow. We must do more than merely catch up. We must become and stay so strong that the Communists will not start an atomic war or allow one to start.
>
> The all-out effort of the Soviets to establish themselves as the masters of the space around us must be met by all-out efforts of our own.

This statement was signed by seventeen Democratic leaders, including former President Harry S Truman, Governor of New York W. Averell Harriman, Adlai Stevenson, Senator Hubert Humphrey, and Senator Herbert Lehman.

Dr. Von Braun noted the bombardment implications of satellites before the Senate Preparedness Subcommittee on December 14, and stated that the United States would be in "mortal danger" if the Russians first gained control of outer space.

Senate Majority Leader Lyndon B. Johnson issued

one of the strongest and most dramatic warnings on space in an important political speech on January 7, 1958:

First, it is obvious that the Soviet valuation on the signifiicance of control of outer space has exceeded that of our officials.

The sputniks now orbiting around the earth are not military weapons, but have a military potential.

Control of space means control of the world, far more certainly, far more totally than any control that has ever or could ever be achieved by weapons, or by troops of occupation.

The race we are in—or which we must enter—is not the race to perfect long-range ballistic missiles. There is something more important than any ultimate weapon. That is the ultimate position—the position of total control over earth lies somewhere out in space.

This is the future, the distant future, though not so distant as we may have thought. Whoever gains that ultimate position gains control, total control, over the earth for purposes of tyranny or for the service of freedom.

Five days later, it became apparent that some of these warnings had begun to create apprehensions in President Eisenhower's mind, when he sent his historic letter of January 12 to Soviet Premier Bulganin:

I propose that we agree that outer space should be used only for peaceful purposes. We face a decisive moment in history in relation to this matter. Both the Soviet Union and the United States are now using outer space for the testing of missiles designed for military purposes. The time to stop is now.

135

Should not outer space be dedicated to the peaceful uses of mankind and denied to the purposes of war? That is my proposal.

On March 15, in their answer to this proposal, the Soviets introduced the first official reference to the orbital bomb concept, and related it to the removal of American foreign bases. It may be that this Soviet statement, coming on top of the many other public warnings such as those noted above, increased administration apprehensions to the point where it was felt that some kind of official reassuring statement on orbital bombardment was needed to avert public panic. In any event, eleven days after the Soviet letter, the President's Science Advisory Committee issued a small circular entitled "Introduction to Outer Space," with a covering letter by President Eisenhower himself. This circular explained in layman's terms some of the basic facts about space, space vehicles and their potential applications. It ended with a direct discussion of orbital bombardment, which will be given here in full, because it was the first statement of a viewpoint to which the United States held with official rigidity thereafter:

> Much has been written about space as a future theater of war, raising such suggestions as satellite bombers, military bases on the moon, and so on. For the most part, even the more sober proposals do not hold up well on close examination or appear to be achievable at an early date. Granted that they will become technologically possible, most of these schemes, nevertheless, appear to be clumsy and ineffective ways of doing a job. Take one example, the satellite as a bomb carrier. A satellite cannot simply drop a bomb. An object released from a satellite doesn't fall. So there is no special advantage in being over the target. Indeed, the only way to "drop" a bomb directly down

136

from a satellite is to carry out aboard the satellite a rocket launching of the magnitude required for an intercontinental missile. A better scheme is to give the weapon to be launched from the satellite a small push, after which it will spiral in gradually. But that means launching it from a moving platform halfway around the world, with every disadvantage compared to a missile based on the ground. In short, the earth would appear to be, after all, the best weapons carrier.

Coming from such an august scientific council, this statement can be interpreted only as an attempt to sweep under the rug the perhaps unpalatable but hard fact that orbital bombardment does hold unique military potential, by avoiding basic facts which would have been obvious to any college engineering student. First, orbital bombs can be made to approach their targets from any direction, which ballistic missiles cannot. Second, a medium-sized "push" can very easily deorbit a bomb only hundreds of miles and two or three minutes from its target, as in the present Soviet FOBS. And third, whereas an earthbound missile base can be identified and photographically inspected from above, it would be far more difficult if not practically impossible to identify and inspect the contents of an orbiting satellite, even if it were close enough to be detected.

Thus, the United States policy which emerged in those days, and which has survived ever since, appears to be one of trying as hard as possible at least to play down, if not to ignore, the military implications of space, perhaps in the hope that in this way the Soviets and later other powers, can be diverted or softly persuaded from extending the armament competition into space. Another objective appears to be withholding as much space authority as possible from the military, because of underlying fears of expanded military influence in American society. More will be said of this later.

Seven days after the Science Advisory Committee's reassurance on orbital bombardment was issued, the emerging United States space policy was set in concrete, when on April 2, 1958, President Eisenhower recommended to the Congress the establishment of a civilian agency, the National Aeronautics and Space Administration (NASA), to control the national space program except for activities of a specifically military nature, which were to be placed under the Department of Defense.

Thus ended the first period of American reaction, a time of shock and confusion. The second period saw NASA wrestling with the problems of getting organized, and a struggle between the advocates of civilian and military control over the roles and missions in space.

As this struggle got underway, it was disclosed by Lieutenant General Bernard A. Schriever, Commander of the Air Force Ballistic Missile Division, on April 24, 1958, in testimony before the House Select Committee on Astronautics and Space Exploration, that the development of military reconnaissance satellites had been given top national priority. This was just six months after Eisenhower's statement that such a thing would not be feasible for a long time. As reported in *The New York Times* for April 25 this project, then named Pied Piper, was to lead to initial test launchings in 1959. It was later called a Satellite and Missile Observation System (SAMOS). It was joined by a second military satellite project to provide early warning of ballistic missile launching, called Missile Defense Alarm System (MIDAS), and a third to develop the capability for satellite interception and inspection (SAINT).

For its part, NASA by October, 1959, had been given

control over the Army's Jet Propulsion Laboratory at Caltech and Dr. Von Braun's rocket team at the Army's Redstone Arsenal in Huntsville, Alabama, as well as several other major research centers. This was the end of the Army's hopes in space, for Von Braun and his team, under Major General John B. Medaris, had been the core of the Army's ballistic missile program.

Increasing pressures from the Air Force and its advocates, for an expanded role in the national space program, surfaced into public view on a number of occasions during the years 1958 through 1961.

Roy W. Johnson, the first head of the Advanced Research Projects Agency (ARPA) under the Eisenhower administration, later declared on February 3, 1960 that civilian control of the space program was "poppycock." He recalled that one of his hardest jobs in the Department of Defense had been trying to convince President Eisenhowever and the "conservative scientists that our space programs should be in the hands of the military and not under civilian control." About two months later, on March 30, he told the House Space Committee that defense leaders still did not appreciate the role space vehicles would play in a war five, ten or fifteen years hence. Specifically, he suggested the committee keep pressing the Pentagon on what it was doing to meet the potential threat that the Soviet Union might be building a "bombardment satellite." Dr. Herbert York, then director of research and engineering in the Department of Defense, questioned the military value of orbital bombardment. He said the Pentagon did not have such capability under development and that he could see no advantage to this means of delivering a warhead over an intercontinental ballistic missile.

Eisenhower's reason for wishing to withhold space

139

authority from the military was strongly hinted at by Dr. Edward C. Welsh, executive secretary of the National Space Council, at a meeting of the Air Force Association in Philadelphia on September 22, 1961. He remarked on the Eisenhower administration's proposed language for the act to create the space agency.

> It was phrased so as not to give clear responsibility to the Department of Defense for space activities primarily associated with military missions. It is possible that this omission was a result of careless drafting or evidence of disinterest in military applications of space or just optimism regarding our military position relative to that of the Communists. In any event, Congress saw the error and changed the language.

(Eisenhower's lack of enthusiasm regarding space in general is indicated in his parting budget message of January 16, 1961: "Further testing and experimentation will be necessary to establish whether there are any valid scientific reasons for extending manned space flight beyond the Mercury program.")

At the same Air Force Association meeting, Representative Emilio Daddario, Trevor Gardner, Dr. Dornberger and General Schriever all emphasized the potential military implications of space weapons. Gardner said, "On August 19, 1960, the USSR placed a 10,120-pound spacecraft in orbit and caused it to land at a time and place of their own choosing. A payload of this size could have been a major nuclear weapon."

Since April, 1959, General Schriever had been responsible for virtually all research and systems development in the Air Force, as head of the Air Force Systems Command. In that position, he was the military leader most

140

closely involved in the civilian-military space controversy. Since 1958, he had publicly voiced criticism of administration policy and management of the space program on a number of occasions, and had called for an expanded Air Force role in space. This struggle reached a turning point in September and October of 1961, immediately after the Soviets broke the test moratorium and exploded their large bombs on the fringes of space. At the Air Force Association meeting in Philadelphia, Schriever stressed the danger that intercontinental missiles could be followed by more destructive space weapons, sooner than most people thought. What was to be his last official comment on the subject was made about three weeks later, on October 12, 1961 at an American Rocket Society meeting in New York City. *The New York Times* reported the next day:

> General Schriever agreed with the Soviet contention that it was possible to put a 100-megaton nuclear weapon (equal to 100,000,000 tons of TNT) into orbit with the rocket that launched the Russian astronauts.
>
> The Air Force research chief insisted that it was 'artificial' to separate peaceful and military research in space.

Apparently this was too much for the administration. The next day, before the same American Rocket Society gathering, Vice President Johnson retorted:

> It is true, of course, that many of the scientific techniques used in civilian research can also be applied to military purposes. But there should be no confusion anywhere about the abiding principles of American policy.

141

We are developing the peaceful uses of outer space from choice, but we are working on the military uses of outer space from necessity.

That difference is basic, not superficial. It is genuine, not artificial. And it is permanent and not temporary.

After that, no further public discussion was heard on the subject from General Schriever or any other official except for periodic presidential reaffirmations that the United States did not expect nuclear weapons to be placed in space. For the most part, the subject of orbital bombardment ceased to exist on the official American scene, until Secretary of Defense McNamara finally announced the development of FOBS in 1967.

In this manner the curtain rang down on the second period of the American reaction, with the military silenced and a peaceful expression stamped on the face of the national space program. Actually, this development might have been sensed five months earlier, when President Kennedy made his first major pronouncement on space since he had taken office. On May 25, 1961, about six weeks after Yuri Gagarin's first manned spaceflight in Vostok 1, Kennedy told the Congress:

Now it is time to take longer strides—time for a great new American enterprise—time for this nation to take a clearly leading role in space achievement which, in many ways, may hold the key to our future on earth.

First, I believe that this nation should commit itself to achieving the goal, before this decade is out, of landing a man on the moon and returning him safely to earth.

It is a most important decision that we make as

142

a nation. But all of you have lived through the last four years and have seen the significance of space and the adventures in space. And no one can predict with certainty what the ultimate meaning will be of the mastery of space.

That Kennedy was uncertain and perhaps disturbed about the strategic implications of space is strongly indicated by this last remark, but that he had a more visionary grasp of the potential of space than Eisenhower had, is evident from the ringing idealism in his historic proposal. That in his space crusade he intended to continue under the peaceful banner that Eisenhower had raised, became finally clear five months later when in an address to the United Nations Assembly, he proposed the seeking of agreements banning nuclear weapons in space. Kennedy's United Nations proposal came only three days after Schriever's and Gardner's warning about space weapons in Philadelphia, and was already history by the time of Schriever's statement on orbital weapons in New York seventeen days later. In view of this timing, the explanation of Vice President Johnson's immediate rebuff to General Schriever is clear.

Six months later, on April 9, 1962, about three weeks after Khrushchev's boast of a global missile, Air Force General Thomas Power, then Commander of the Strategic Air Command, made a last plea for the extension of SAC's mission to space, and for development of the manned space vehicles which would be required. One day later, a Department of Defense security directive was announced which placed rigid restrictions on what information could be released about the department's satellite launchings, and with that the whole subject of reconnaissance satellites, the names SAMOS, MIDAS and SAINT, and official mention of military activities in space as such,

143

ceased abruptly, as had discussion of orbital bombardment
five months earlier.

The third period of American reaction to Soviet
space initiatives, which has extended from 1961 to the
present, still carries the imprint of the Kennedy policy,
which is to maintain a primarily nonmilitary interpretation of the national space program, while developing basic
space capabilities using the Apollo lunar landing project
as a spearhead and focus. Shortly after Sokolovskii's remarks on space were published in Moscow, Kennedy re-
affirmed this policy in clear terms in a speech at Rice
University on September 12, 1962, at which time he again
saw fit to express reassurance on the orbital bomb issue.

> We choose to go to the moon in this decade—
> because that goal will serve to organize and measure
> the best of our energies and skills; because that chal-
> lenge is one we're willing to accept; one we are un-
> willing to postpone, and one that we intend to win.
> We have vowed that we shall not see space filled
> with weapons of mass destruction but with instru-
> ments of knowledge and understanding. Yet the vows
> of this nation can only be fulfilled if we in this nation
> are first and therefore we intend to be first.

Despite these and earlier efforts of the Eisenhower
and Kennedy administrations to play down the potential
value of strategic space systems and to divert attention
toward non-military activities, it is evident that thought-
ful individuals outside the government were beginning to
ponder the other side of the matter. For example, in the
book *Outer Space in World Politics*, published early in
1963, some penetrating comments on the subject were
recorded by two eminent strategic analysts, Professor
Thomas Schelling of Harvard and Professor Klaus Knorr,

144

Director of the Center of International Studies at Princeton. Schelling stated:

> It is widely taken for granted that nuclear weapons in orbit would be a bad thing, bad for both us and the Russians if we both had them, and that their prohibition is obviously desirable if we can negotiate it and monitor it in a reliable way. The unquestioning acceptance of that view is undoubtedly based partly on intellectual laziness, on a failure to analyse the bombardment satellite on its own merits.

Schelling noted further that adding the space dimension to the strategic picture might not only "ease the problem of protecting a retaliatory force," but also "add significant worries to the political leader who has to take responsibility for initiating an attack." He continued:

> Some of the above remarks suggest that the military use of outer space, or at least the use of outer space for actual launching platforms, might favor stability rather than instability. In that case, according to certain important criteria of arms control, one would not want to ban this use of space.

Professor Knorr commented:

> If the safety of the earth's systems leaves something to be desired, bomb satellites will augment deterrent safety either by being less vulnerable than terrestrial components or, if equally or somewhat more vulnerable, by providing deterrent diversity, thereby complicating any potential attack and thus upgrading the overall capability to deter.
> The most probable contingencies are that bomb satellites either will have little military significance

or will add to the stability of a system of relatively secure deterrent forces in which case, again, the control of lesser aggression through the threat of strategic retaliation will lack credibility. For the same reason, it is probable that conflicts arising in outer space will not touch off a round of mutual annihilation on earth.

Later in his article, Schelling did acknowledge that a ban on strategic weapons in space might be desirable from certain points of view, as a symbolic step toward relieving tensions, and as a precedent for further agreements between the great powers. Yet there can be no mistaking both his and Knorr's appeal that the question of the strategic implications of space should be taken up on a sober, objective basis, with all sides considered, and not as an emotional issue. This appeal went unheeded by the United States government and no open, objective dialogue on the subject ever occurred.

Instead, Kennedy pressed his crusade for peaceful space activity to the extreme of inviting the Soviet Union to join the United States in the lunar landing program, in a speech to the United Nations General Assembly on September 20, 1963. The President was assassinated two months later, so the Soviets had little chance to respond to such a monumental proposal, if they ever had any inclination to do so.

The momentum of his efforts continued after his death, however, and in December of that year, the United Nations issued its seventeen-nation resolution on the banning of nuclear weapons from space, the main provisions of which were later embodied in the Space Treaty of 1967. Thus, it is not surprising that the insights of Knorr, Schelling and others have gone largely unnoticed.

146

On December 10, 1963, cancellation of the Air Force Dyna-Soar manned orbital vehical project was announced. This effort, since being approved in 1957 after Dr. Dornberger's six-year promotion, had during the six further years of its existence received no approval for the heavy funding necessary to construct and flight-test a prototype, but had produced much in the way of basic technology needed for such vehicles. It was replaced immediately with a two-man orbital "can" or station, to be used for testing purposes and referred to as the Manned Orbiting Laboratory (MOL), to be first launched in 1967 or 1968. In announcing this project, Secretary McNamara said it would be used "to supply information on navigation aids and metallurgical questions, as well as other classified projects." Only token funding was provided for MOL, however, and the project was to languish for nearly two years before final go-ahead.

The Kennedy space policy was continued through the Johnson administration with little if any change. It continued to be reactive. On September 15, 1964, Khrushchev made his boast about a "monstrous new terrible weapon" that could destroy mankind. Three days later, President Johnson made public the fact that the United States had assembled on Johnson Island in the Pacific Ocean, a pilot installation for an antisatellite missile system capable of intercepting and destroying hostile satellites. He also said the United States was working on an over-the-horizon radar which would permit detection of hostile satellites as soon as they were launched. He coupled these statements with another reassurance about orbital weapons: "We have no reason to believe that any nation plans to put nuclear warheads into orbit."

On July 3, 1965, Soviet Communist Party Leader Brezhnev made his threatening statement about "intercontinental and orbital rockets." About six weeks later, President Johnson announced full funding for a go-ahead on MOL, including flight tests then expected in 1969 or 1970. The purposes of MOL he stated as follows:

> This program will bring us new knowledge about what man is able to do in space. It will enable us to relate that ability to the defense of America. It will develop technology and equipment which will help advance manned and unmanned space flight and it will make it possible to perform very new and rewarding experiments with that technology and equipment.

Johnson strained to preserve the peaceful aura by again reaffirming the United States commitment not to place weapons in space, and even went so far as to invite the U.S.S.R. Academy of Sciences to send a representative to observe the December, 1965 launch of Gemini VI. The response was immediate and appeared on the same day in *Krasnaya Zvezda*: "The main purpose is testing the capability of intercepting artificial satellites and conducting reconnaissance from space." The Soviet interpretation of MOL was stated even more strongly about two weeks later on September 9 in an article by Col. Gen. Vladimir Tolubko, Deputy Commander in Chief of the Strategic Rocket Forces:

> Now the Pentagon wants to use space laboratories not only for espionage but also to accomplish direct combat tasks. Is it possible that the Pentagon generals intend to drop conventional bombs from outer space? Of course not. Surely, nothing but nuclear bombs are implied.
> All this does not tally with President Johnson's hypocritical announcement about extending the rule of law to outer space.

148

Perhaps President Johnson was stung by this remark, and certainly he was beset by the problems of trying to find the funds to support simultaneously a growing war in Vietnam, his "Great Society" projects, and a national space program. In any event on May 7, 1966, he called for resumption of negotiations for a treaty to prohibit mass destruction weapons from space, which had been interrupted by the Berlin and Cuban crises. That Johnson was uneasy about the strategic portents of space, as Kennedy had been before him, was indicated in the wording of his request for negotiations:

> I am convinced that we should do what we can—not only for our generation but for future generations—to see to it that serious political conflicts do not arise as a result of space activities. I believe that the time is ripe for action. We should not lose time.

Four months later, General Schriever retired from the Air Force. Shortly thereafter, on November 30, 1966, at a meeting in Boston of the American Institute of Aeronautics and Astronautics, he expressed himself again. *The New York Times* reported that day:

> The man who spearheaded the development of America's ballistic missile arsenal warned here today that the nation cannot ignore the threat of manned military aggression in outer space.
> General Bernard A. Schriever, who retired in September as Commander of the Air Force Systems Command, said that international treaties, though desirable, could not be relied on to prevent space from becoming a battleground or a new 'high ground' for attacks on earth bases.

The Space Treaty was signed on January 27, 1967

and went into effect on October 10 of that year. MOL continued to lag further behind schedule as a result of budget reductions and was finally canceled on June 5, 1969. Its place was taken in late July of that year by the NASA-three man Orbiting Workshop scheduled for first launch in 1972. Thus, in manned space station technology, the United States by 1969, lagged more than three years behind the Soviets, who, as noted in Chapter III, assembled their first manned station in January, 1969. This fact should be kept in mind during the subsequent discussion of deterrence and technological surprise.

Meanwhile, just two days before signing the Space Treaty, the Soviets had begun flight-testing FOBS, and on November 3, 1967, 24 days after the Space Treaty took effect, Mr. McNamara announced its existence to the American people at a news conference in the Pentagon:

> I would like today to discuss with you certain intelligence information we have collected on a series of space system flight tests being conducted by the Soviet Union. These relate to the possible development by the Soviet of something we have called a fractional orbital bombardment system, or FOBS.
> Even now it is impossible to be certain of what these tests represent. It is conceivable that the Soviet Union has been testing space vehicles for some re-entry program. But we suspect that the Russians are pursuing the research and development of a FOBS. If this turns out to be true, it is conceivable that they could achieve an initial operational capability during 1968.

He went on to describe FOBS as a system to place 1-3 megaton bombs in orbit at about 100 miles altitude, from which they could be deorbited approximately 500 miles

150

and three minutes before striking their targets. He noted that this country, anticipating such a capability, had begun to deploy over-the-horizon (OTH) radars which could give fifteen minutes warning of an approaching FOBS, about the same warning as is possible of a ballistic missile attack, by the Ballistic Missile Early Warning System (BMEWS).

In view of the history recounted here, this announcement should have come as no surprise, for it is evident that bombardment from space, together with large warheads, are capabilities which have long occupied an important place in Soviet military development and planning.

Nor should it be surprising, in view of the often-stated United States space policy, that Mr. McNamara should have attempted to depreciate FOBS, both as a possible Soviet strategic threat and as an undermining of the Space Treaty. But his attempts seemed even less convincing than those of President Eisenhower's Science Advisory Committee nearly ten years earlier. Mr. McNamara made six points:

First, that because of limited payload and accuracy, FOBS would not be effective against hard targets such as Minuteman missiles in their silos, but might be intended for more vulnerable targets such as U.S. bomber bases. (This in itself is a formidable threat, but might the current FOBS not be merely a test version leading to much larger bombs in orbit, and should not accuracy be expected to improve with advancing technology?)

Second, that OTH gives sufficient warning of approaching FOBS to wash out any advantages of surprise. (Even if OTH or other kinds of warning systems operating from satellites, do give fifteen, thirty, or even sixty minutes warning of approach, attack is not confirmed

151

until deorbit three minutes before the target is hit. If decoys were launched repeatedly or left up for multiple orbits, could they not impose a continuous, prohibitively costly alert on U.S. bomber forces? How could it be determined whether supposedly peaceful orbiting satellites were not actually bombs?)

Third, that even if the Soviets put bombs in continuous orbits for surprise deorbit on three minute warning, too large a number would be required for the system to be effective. (Could not multiple warheads, or MIRV, be employed on orbital weapons as they are on ballistic missiles, thus reducing the number required?)

Fourth, that the United States years ago studied the desirability of developing a FOBS, decided there was no need, and has no intention of reversing that decision. (Should the lack of a U.S. requirement years ago preclude the development of such a requirement now or in the future?)

Fifth, that "As you know, our deterrent rests upon our ability to absorb any surprise attack and to retaliate with sufficient strength to destroy the attacking nation as a viable society. With three minutes warning, fifteen minutes warning or no warning at all, we could still absorb a surprise attack and strike back with enough power to destroy the attacker. We have that capability today; we will continue to have it in the future." (How long would the United States have this retaliatory capability, if the Soviets could develop a surprise means of negating first the bomber forces, and perhaps eventually a certain portion of the missile forces through larger or multiple warheads and improved accuracy?)

Sixth, the FOBS is not a violation of the Space Treaty, because it would not be in orbit for a full circuit of the earth. This point has since been amplified by certain State and Defense Department officials, who point

152

out that FOBS can be considered equivalent to a ballistic missile, except only that it utilizes an orbital rather than a ballistic flight path.

This sixth point avoids the fact that, unlike a ballistic missile, an orbital bomb of any sort, including FOBS, requires a separate deorbit firing action to make its attack from orbit, so that the orbital portion of its flight is in some ways like a super-ready deployment phase rather than an attack phase as is a ballistic trajectory. Also, the view that an object is not in orbit unless it has completed a full earth circuit is technically unsound, and an unwarranted warping of Space Treaty wording, the intention of which is quite unambiguous. The only reasonable and honest conclusion is that FOBS is a weapon which, while not violating the Space Treaty by its existence, could not perform its delivery and attack mission without violating the treaty, and is therefore not in keeping with the spirit of the treaty. In short, the Soviet development of FOBS, and the United States defense of their right to do so under the Space Treaty, surely is a serious undermining of the treaty and must raise grave doubt about the degree to which such a treaty should be relied upon to prevent expansion of the arms competition into space.

The official U.S. interpretation, therefore, raised a number of disturbing questions. A more ominous question, however loomed in the background: Why had the Soviets, who had shown themselves clearly capable of establishing coherent missile and space objectives, and formulating and executing effective programs for their achievement, gone to the effort and expense of developing space bombardment capability, if it is as inconsequential as the initial U.S. interpretation suggested? Why would the Soviets for ten years have repeatedly hinted at and even announced outright their development of orbital bombs, perhaps encountering a major failure with the

Scrag as has been suggested, only to try again, if there were not sound reasons for their so doing? It would appear either that the Soviet military and space planners were in gross error, which is a risky assumption in view of their past record, that their U.S. counterparts were in gross error, which seems unlikely, or that the official U.S. announcement was specifically designed to play down the implications of bombardment from space, to avert public anxiety and avoid an escalation of the arms race.

In the light of this review of American reactions during the first decade of the Soviet space initiative, some important facts jump into perspective.

It is clear that American space policy has been to assume strongly an orientation toward space as an arena for peaceful activity, while diverting attention from its undoubtedly real strategic implications. It has attempted to obscure the military importance of space by direct statement denying the value of orbital bombardment (from the President's Science Advisory Committee in 1958 to State and Defense Department comments on FOBS in 1967 and 1968), and by imposing secrecy in 1962 on military satellite programs which account for a very significant portion of all U.S. space launchings. Execution of this policy has been made easier by independent influences such as scientists and others who fear the effects of a military-dominated space program, and developments such as the Vietnam War and domestic urban problems which compete for funds. It has been made harder by the existence of military space spokesmen and military satellite programs, both of which have had to be silenced.

Just as it is clear what posture American space policy has attempted to strive for, it is also clear that the harder facts of reality show through, when a perspective view is taken. As seen above, specific cases have shown repeatedly that the national space program has been primarily a

154

reactive one to outside events, particularly to Soviet statements and developments about orbital bombardment. The most substantial initiative taken by the United States was President Kennedy's launching of the Apollo lunar landing program which would develop basic capabilities for manned operations in deep space. Yet Apollo itself must be regarded as a reaction, not only to Gagarin's Vostok 1 flight, but even more to the humiliation suffered by the United States in the abortive invasion at the Bay of Pigs in Cuba, just a month earlier.

Despite frequent professions to the contrary, uncertainty and uneasiness about the strategic implications of space have repeatedly shown through official statements, from the Democratic Advisory Council's and Johnson's statements just after Sputnik 1, to Kennedy's proposal of Apollo in Congress, and Johnson's call for an outer space treaty in 1966. Finally, official U.S. statements minimizing the military value of orbital bombardment have been very unconvincing.

Thus, while the Soviets have been developing space weapons, the United States government has tried as hard as possible to look the other way, sweeping under the carpet considerations which are unsettling but of critical importance, apparently in hopes that these considerations would fade away or go unnoticed. This policy could have dramatic implications for the future. It could bring on worse troubles in the long run than it averts in the short, especially in an era when technological surprise can have decisive impact.

DETERRENCE AND TECHNOLOGICAL SURPRISE

There are several reasons to expect that any nation, and especially the United States, will be increasingly subject to the possibility of technological surprise, as time goes on.

A major reason is the strategy of deterrence itself, particularly as it is widely understood and interpreted in the United States. This strategy may be stated as that of maintaining a credible "second strike" capability, which means being able to absorb the heaviest blow an attacker can deliver, and having sufficient forces surviving to deliver an unacceptably heavy strike in return. The strategy also entails neither side achieving a "first strike" capability, which means the capacity to strike a heavy enough first blow to wipe out the possibility of effective retaliation. The deterrent policy of the United States, and its strategic position relative to that of the Soviet Union, was summed up by Secretary of Defense McNamara on September 18, 1967:

> The blunt fact is, then, that neither the Soviet Union nor the United States can attack the other without being destroyed in retaliation; nor can either of us attain a first-strike capability in the foreseeable future.
>
> The further fact is that both the Soviet Union and the United States presently possess an actual and credible second-strike capability against one another—and it is precisely this mutual capability that provides us both with the strongest possible motive to avoid a nuclear war.

This situation has been called "stable" deterrence, in which the chance of miscalculation by a potential attacker is reduced essentially to zero, and the probability of nuclear war is shrunk to the irreducible minimum associated with accident or irresponsibility. It is often implied that once such a "stable" deterrent is achieved, it is against the mutual interest, and therefore undesirable and un-necessary, to expend effort on development of new stra-tegic capabilities such as more survivable or destructive force delivery, or improved defense, since such develop-ments would "de-stabilize" the strategic balance and lead to an escalation of the arms competition. Thus, in the United States, emphasis has been focused on increasing the numbers, and to some degree the effectiveness, of exist-ing strategic missile systems such as Minuteman and Posei-don, and prolonging the effectiveness of manned bombers. Support has been diverted from new "de-stabilizing" de-velopments, such as strategic space systems and missile defense, which finally was authorized in a limited version in September, 1967, but only reluctantly and with the claim that it was oriented toward Communist China and not the Soviet Union.

The United States reluctance to embark on develop-ment of strategic space systems has been seen in the pre-ceding history, and was stated outright by Deputy Secre-tary of Defense Roswell Gilpatrick in September, 1962, about six months after Khrushchev's announcement of a global missile, and about the time that Marshal Sokolov-skii's book was published: "An arms race in space will not contribute to our security. I can think of no greater stim-ulus for a Soviet thermonuclear arms effort in space than a United States commitment to such a program. This we will not do."

There are strong reasons to think, however, that in reality there cannot exist even an approximation to a truly stable condition where "de-stabilizing" developments can be avoided. As emphasized in Chapter I, the advance of technology is inescapable, and it would appear utopian to expect any major power to withhold from utilizing new knowledge for weapon improvement and development. As

157

we have seen, United States restraint in developing new "de-stabilizing" space systems certainly has not dissuaded the Soviets from pushing ahead on new and portentous space capabilities of their own. This has always been so, and realistic strategic planning has to allow for it. The only new aspect is that technology is advancing more rapidly than ever, and that new developments in both offense and defense can be expected with increasing rapidity. Belief that "stable" deterrence can be maintained at fixed levels of technology for more than very short times, in the face of such rapid technical advance, is potentially hazardous. Policies of reluctance to develop new military capabilities on ground they are "de-stabilizing" and on hopes that the other side will act likewise, have been criticized widely, perhaps with some justification, as something approaching unilateral arms reduction. These considerations are especially relevant to the development of space systems, where programs must be undertaken five to ten years in advance of the desired capabilities, with the result that technological surprise in this field could be decisive.

Appreciation of this fact was indicated clearly in Secretary McNamara's statement of September 18, 1967:

> How can we be so certain that the Soviets cannot gradually outdistance us—either by some dramatic technology breakthrough or simply through our imperceptibility lagging behind, for whatever reason: reluctance to spend the requisite funds; distraction with military problems elsewhere; faulty intelligence; or simple negligence and naiveté?
>
> The answer to all this is simple and straightforward.
>
> We are not going to permit the Soviets to outdistance us, because to do so would be to jeopardize our very stability as a nation.

We do not want a nuclear arms race with the Soviet Union. But if the only way to prevent the Soviet Union from obtaining first-strike capability over us is to engage in such a race, the United States possesses in ample abundance the resources, the technology and the will to run faster in that race for whatever distance is required.

Although this statement may be somewhat difficult to reconcile with McNamara's reassurances about FOBS less than two months later, it is still a clear recognition of the problem of technological surprise. It is an indication of growing official awareness of the vulnerability which can result from closed-mind attitudes toward new military systems, because they are thought to be destabilizing.

A second important reason for increasing vulnerability to technological surprise is the fact that in this era of ever more rapid technical advances, important developments can be made under cover of sufficient secrecy that intelligence about them is difficult if not impossible to acquire. For example, the development, testing and installation of MIRV warheads on ballistic missiles or orbital rockets might be accomplished with few outward signs, such as special facilities or telltale vehicle features, which could be detected by reconnaissance. The same might be true of decoys and other devices to aid penetration of warning and defense systems. And, when laboratories are placed in space, especially in deep space where they would be extremely difficult to detect and monitor, many clandestine military experiments, developments and operations may be carried out. The first power to achieve a "death ray" weapon may derive much of the critical development and test information from a laser laboratory in space.

Another factor which increases the likelihood of technological surprise is the incursion of outside events which divert attention and compete for funds. For example, many commentators who react most readily to the visible and the immediate, have been strongly critical of the space program for draining funds away from other worthwhile causes such as improved educational, medical and welfare services. These criticisms for the most part do not consider the question whether the funds would actually be made available for these other purposes, even if the space program didn't exist at all. These criticisms also ignore the historical experience that nations which slight their technological development in favor of social programs, may tend to lose rapidly their vitality as world powers. A current example is England, whose drift into welfarism has been accompanied by a precipitous decline in global influence since World War II. By contrast, the Soviet Union and Communist China which, for all their talk of socialist morality, have placed higher priority on military and technological programs than on consumer welfare, have risen dramatically in the international power structure.

Far more serious has been the effect of the war in Vietnam, which has been a direct influence in reducing the United States expenditures on space from 7.7 billion dollars in fiscal 1966, to 6.1 billion in fiscal 1970. This represents a decrease from about one percent to somewhat over one half of one percent of the Gross National Product. And this at a time when, according to a study prepared by twelve agencies of the Johnson administration and reported to Congress on January 30, 1968, the Soviets were giving higher priority than the United States to their space program, in terms of level of expenditures. In view of these developments the natural question has been raised more than once: Might not a major objective of

160

Soviet support for the Vietnam War be precisely that of diverting U.S. attention and funds away from space activities and development, perhaps buying time to build a foundation for some kind of technological surprise in space?

The threat of technological surprise has thus become established as a fact of life, and is likely to loom even larger in the future, as the pace of technology quickens. In this environment, the stability of deterrence can be maintained only if constant efforts are made to keep strategic posture fully abreast of new knowledge rather than merely responding to potential threats as they actually become apparent. This points away from the so-called stable deterrence which, in its usual interpretation as discussed above probably should be called "static," to a more flexible form which might better be called "dynamic deterrence." Deterrence must be technologically dynamic in nature if the strategic balance is to be maintained, particularly if options are to be kept open to utilize the unprecedented military value of space, if and when that is necessary. This is equivalent to saying that nations are wise to arm themselves to meet a competitor's possible capabilities rather than his apparent intentions, because intentions can be hidden or altered, but the competitor cannot easily surpass or surprise in capability, a nation which is alert and technologically aggressive.

It seems certain that these facts cannot but be fully realized not only by the United States and the Soviet Union, but by the other major powers as well, and that, as a result, nations which are able to do so will inevitably avail themselves of every opportunity to go to space and to utilize space to whatever degree is possible and necessary, for purposes of national security. If this develops

161

to be the case, and the facts certainly seem to favor it, then the next question is how might the present state of affairs evolve toward the ultimate extension of strategic capabilities into the space arena?

SPECULATIONS ABOUT THE FUTURE

At least four factors in world events have emerged from this discussion, which must be considered of great importance as underlying influences which will help shape the future of the armaments competition and man's activities in space. They are the technological erosion of the survivability of earthbound strategic systems, the Soviet drive for space weapons and the emergence of FOBS, the developing capabilities for deep-space operations in the form of the Apollo program and its Soviet counterpart, and the growing necessity for continuing forward with new technologies to avoid being outdistanced or surprised.

All of these factors point toward a gradually escalating race between the United States and the Soviet Union to explore, develop and utilize new systems to extend strategic capabilities into space. Exactly how this race could develop step by step is impossible to tell until the events themselves begin to take shape. But the existence of the above four influences, all pointing in the same direction, justifies a certain degree of speculation on the future.

Already, as a result of new techniques such as improved reconnaissance, penetrability, multiple warheads, high-yield bombs, underwater detection and other forms of antisubmarine warfare, it appears probable that before many years Minuteman missiles and Polaris-Poseidon submarines will go the way of the manned bomber. For example, the eroding impact of multiple independently-targetable reentry vehicles (MIRV) on the survivability of

162

silo-based land missiles, is indicated by the following Pentagon statement of January 16, 1968: "Each new MIRV warhead will be aimed individually, and will be more accurate than any previous or existing warhead. They will be far better suited for destruction of hardened missile sites than any existing missile warheads." While this may have sounded reassuring, it must be presumed not only that the Soviets also have, or soon will have, comparable capability against U.S. missiles, but that the Soviet MIRV might be utilized along FOBS trajectories. Such enhanced counterforce surprise attack capability in the hands of a potential attacker would be a most ominous development.

It has been suggested that the demise of land-based missile systems could be delayed a short while by such measures as making them rail-mobile, road-mobile, or off-road mobile, and shuffling them in large numbers at random about one's own land mass, but this is a makeshift and very costly solution, and probably would tend to compound rather than alleviate the question of collateral damage hazard to populations. In addition, such systems would be easy targets for saboteurs and hijackers. It has also been suggested that missile silos be further hardened, and that entire missile systems be deployed inside mountains or deep in the thousands of miles of abandoned hard rock mines which exist in certain sections of the country. In each of these approaches, however, the doors through which the missiles are launched must still be on the surface, visible to reconnaissance, and increasingly vulnerable to MIRV, higher bomb yields and improving attack accuracies, even as are the doors of Minuteman silos.

Active defense using some variant of the Safeguard anti-ballistic missile system provides a further alternative for attempting to protect land-based strategic missiles against massive coordinated attacks such as from MIRV. As noted previously, however, the technical feasibility of effective defense against attacks employing salvos or decoys, is extremely doubtful. And there has been much expert testimony that the classic advantages of offense over defense manifest themselves once again in this modern situation, in that it is easier and cheaper for the attacker to salvo, decoy or otherwise add complexity to his attack, than it is for the defender to increase the sophistication of his defense system, to handle that complexity.

The increasing vulnerability of undersea operations to detection and attack is hinted in the following statement by *The New York Times* for May 11, 1968:

> Pentagon sources are reluctant to provide too detailed a picture of the means by which they keep track of Soviet submarines for fear of giving the Russians information on which to base countermeasures.
>
> It is known, however, that a global network of air, surface and subsurface systems is employed to try to keep tabs on the comings and goings of Soviet vessels.

An article in *Time* magazine for February 23, 1968, was even more specific in discussing means by which near-orbit satellite sensors can scan the oceans to detect the heat and turbulence of submarine wakes, and underwater networks of listening devices that can pick up electronic "signatures" given off by subs. The article states: "Through such systems, the U.S. Navy is able to track Soviet subs with uncanny accuracy throughout most of the world's waters." If the United States has these kinds of techniques, it must be expected that the Soviets also will develop them before long.

Even if it is still in a primitive state of development, the capability to monitor the activities of other powers throughout the water masses of the oceans casts grave long-term doubts on the survivability and strategic effectiveness not only of missile-launching ships and submarines, but of more advanced concepts as well, such as missiles deployed on the ocean floor. The danger of Pueblo-type boarding and seizure on the high seas would be particularly acute for missile-launching surface ships, and foreign inspection or capture of the classified equipment and armament aboard them, could be disastrous to national security.

In the face of such developments, it is only to be expected that a deterrent power will seek more effective ways of ensuring the survivability of its strategic forces, and that a potential attacker will redouble his efforts to find new and better systems for surprise attack. FOBS is such a surprise attack system, for it could increase the complexity of obtaining warning of its approach by its relatively low altitude and multidirectional attack, and of defense because of the delay of attack confirmation until three minutes before the target is hit. (Of course, the usual question could be raised, "Why wait until the last minute, or until we are hit, before launching a retaliatory strike? Why not launch on warning?" Strong arguments can be made against launch-on-warning, however, on grounds that such a policy could lead quickly and easily to hair-trigger, unstable alert conditions in which an accidental, miscalculated or irresponsible nuclear exchange could all too readily result.) Because of these new and unique features of FOBS, it becomes itself another of the evolving technology areas such as recon-

165

naissance, antisubmarine warfare, guidance accuracy and multiple warheads—improvements in which relentlessly erode the survivability of earthbound strategic deterrent systems.

It does not require much imagination to see more ominous implications of FOBS. As already noted, the future of the Space Treaty must be regarded with some skepticism. In view of this, it is not irrelevant to speculate on the possible repercussions of the employment of a multiple or continuously orbiting bombardment system in near orbit, a capability claimed for Scrag, and which is almost certainly inherent in FOBS. Such a situation could grow serious indeed. It could be particularly difficult for the United States if it had developed no detection or inspection capability, to determine whether claimed Soviet bomb satellites really were bombs, and whether supposedly unarmed satellites actually were not bombs. Dependable inspection systems, manned or unmanned, might not even be feasible if it were found that effective booby-trapping were possible. Such a situation could lead to unstable confusion, where large numbers of satellites and decoys, some carrying bombs and some not, circle the earth in a profusion of orbits, with no one certain which is which.

It might be argued that the chain of events leading to such a catastrophe need not be allowed to start. Because of the vulnerability to ground fire of objects in near-orbit space, antisatellite missile sites or airborne mobile launch platforms probably could be deployed underneath likely orbital paths, relatively easily and rapidly, to deny near-orbit overflight of any desired territory by potential attackers. Just as the United States did not permit deployment of Soviet missiles in Cuba, 90 miles off the tip of Florida, it seems just as likely that it would not be willing

166

to permit their deployment in near-orbit space where they could come within 100 miles of any point in the United States. But if inspection techniques were not available, would the United States fire on a suspected bomb in orbit if it had been announced, say, as a research satellite?

As concluded in Chapter II, the future of jurisdiction and strategic competition in near-orbit space must remain an open issue, to be decided by the manner in which events work themselves out. Certain underlying considerations, however, suggest that some equilibrium may emerge, short of the above extreme alternative: 1) the obvious provocativeness of near-orbit overflight by mass destructive weapons; 2) the vulnerability of near-orbit satellites to ground fire; 3) the relatively large and complex system of weapons required for continuous earth target coverage from near-orbit space, and 4) the risks of malfunction, accidental attack, espionage and sabotage to weapons left in orbit unattended for long periods. There would seem to be reason to hope that these factors will inhibit a potential attacker from willy-nilly instigating a chaos of continuously orbiting unknowns and permanent hair-trigger alert conditions, however tempting the features of surprise which might be offered.

It appears far more likely that FOBS, as well as being a surprise attack component of Soviet strategic forces, will in addition serve as a testbed to develop the technological know-how necessary to place bombs in space, to maintain them there in safety and readiness, and to deorbit them accurately toward their targets. This know-how could later be transferred to deep-space systems, when the vehicles and equipment necessary for deep-space operations become available.

The first generation of such vehicles and equipment has been developed by the United States, in the Apollo lunar landing program. This program will provide, by the early 1970's, the Saturn V launch vehicle, which can place nearly fifty tons in deep space; the Apollo Command Module which can serve as a three-man shuttle between the earth and orbits in deep space, and the Lunar Module, which can land on and take off from the moon with two men aboard. These vehicles, their associated equipment, and the experience gained from deep-space flight and lunar exploration, will provide a sound technological base for the development of strategic space systems which could be undertaken well before 1980. Indeed, as mentioned in Chapter III, development of the key building blocks for such systems, particularly a flexible manned shuttle vehicle as a successor to the Command Module, could be undertaken on the basis of today's technology, and appears to be a logical next step.

The Soviets, from all reports, are approaching comparable capabilities and should be sufficiently advanced technically to begin development of strategic space systems, at about the same time as the United States.

At that time the Space Treaty, if it is still a living instrument, will face increasingly severe tests of its viability. Since it contains no provisions for enforcement, or even for inspection of launch operations and orbiting objects, adherence to the treaty must be by faith and trust alone, unless inspection provisions are added, which seems unlikely judging from historic Soviet reluctance about inspection. An important fact here is the character of the Soviet national space program, in which no administrative distinction is made between military and nonmilitary activity, and in which the military apparently plays a very active role. In a time when manned space flights are made with increasing frequency, and it is not known just where they are going or what they are doing out there, it seems very unlikely that either the United States or the Soviet Union would not take the precaution of quietly developing its strategic space capabilities so as not to be vulnerable to surprise attack, or to some kind of technological Pearl Harbor.

Sometime after 1980, it can be expected that other industrial nations will have grown technically and economically to the point where they, also, will be able to build and operate strategic space systems. How might the development of such systems be expected to evolve, and with what consequences?

Two primary possibilities appear to exist. Deep-space military forces may be developed either unilaterally, or by two powers approximately simultaneously, by agreement or competition. If they are developed unilaterally, the purpose may be either deterrence or aggression. If it is deterrence, then deterrence will be strengthened and any potential aggressor would be forced into space if he wished to retain any chance at all of eventually altering the deterrent situation. If it is aggression, then the danger of surprise attack will increase and it is unlikely that the United States or any other deterrent power would allow such a unilateral capability to arise.

Deep-space strategic forces could be developed by two powers nearly simultaneously, and it now seems very likely that this could evolve from the present space competition between the United States and the Soviet Union. If by that time the Soviet Union were clearly a deterrent rather than a potentially aggressive power (as a result, for example, of continuing and increasing concern about the threat of a growing Communist China), then the deterrent situation would be stabilized, at least until other powers also developed strategic space capabilities.

If the Soviet Union were to be regarded as a potential

169

attacker, however, then, as early perhaps as the late 1970's, the spectacle would arise of two hostile strategic forces deployed in deep space. Within the confines of foreseeable technology, both forces probably would at first be practically invulnerable to detection and attack from earth or space, and both would be capable of inflicting nearly complete surprise against soft and perhaps some hard earthbound targets. In this situation, since the deterrent power would have little or no knowledge of the location of the aggressor's strike forces, he could achieve deterrence only by targeting the potential attacker's cities and populations, and for the same reason the potential attacker must be expected to do likewise.

At this point, it is natural to ask, "Why deploy deterrent forces in space, if that can only increase the incentive for both sides to target cities? What is gained thereby?" It is true that the basic strategic situation would not be changed fundamentally, but there is a distinct benefit in that while the aggressor might be capable of complete surprise against targets on earth, he can no longer inflict any degree of damage at all against strategic deterrent forces in deep space, if he doesn't know where they are. Even if he does know where they are, if he tries to attack them from earth, by that action he will give advanced warning of his attack. The stability of deterrence would thus be enhanced. This is a step in the right direction in view of the fact that advancing technology is constantly eroding the survivability of earthbound forces and thus degrading the stability of deterrence based on them.

The second step, which is the reduction of the incentive to target earthbound populations, can be achieved only after significant forces are already deployed in space, and after those forces eventually gain the technological capability to target each other. As emphasized previously, if counterforce capability exists, the motivations to target noncombatants tend to be diminished. Counterforce between deep-space systems, however, must await detection, tracking and surveillance capabilities which still lie in the future.

Eventually, however, advancing technology will very likely produce effective methods for detecting and attacking targets in increasingly large volumes of space, and also of defending them. When that happens, there will be a growing premium on maneuverability, shielding, and both offensive and defensive space weapons, and the space stations of tomorrow could evolve into "battle cruisers" of the day after.

In that more distant era, the focus of strategic conflict might at last shift away from the earth, and into space. Then the kind of deterrent situation presently existing between earthbound ballistic missile forces, though not changed fundamentally, may have been at least partially transferred to space, creating at last a realistic possibility of alleviating the threat to earthbound populations, from the proximity of weapons for mass destruction. While this transference cannot be regarded as a complete guarantee that all city targeting will cease, it probably would reduce the numbers of population and cities held hostage, and ensure that in any actual exchange of nuclear blows, much of the megatonnage would be expended in space, thus avoiding not only prompt destruction on earth, but also strontium 90 and other delayed radioactive fallout effects.

In attempts such as this to project possible futures, it must be borne in mind that in the past such projections have often foundered on the rocks of technological breakthroughs or other unforeseen developments sufficiently dramatic and fundamental to have changed basic ground

171

rules. Many of these surprises have been relatively sudden, and there is no reason to expect that similar events will not occur in the future. For example, unilateral development by a potential aggressor, of improved attack or defense methods against ballistic or space weapons, perhaps using radiation beam techniques or something like the much-discussed "neutron bomb" which could destroy life without destroying real estate, might invalidate deterrence and suddenly increase the danger of surprise attack. This is only one of several possibilities which provide a powerful incentive to explore constantly all technical areas as a hedge against such surprises.

The actual course of events thus cannot be predicted in detail and may diverge from the above speculations. Yet such is the uncertainty of life, and this should not be allowed to discourage serious evaluation of potential futures, or delay the beginning of the development of whatever key capabilities appear necessary to keep open desirable options.. With regard to strategic space systems, development would have to be undertaken long before the capability could be achieved, and with the recognition that in the meanwhile there may be turnings of the road.

At this point in time, however, there appears to be increasing promise that the prospects of both survivability and surprise in deep space could lead first to an extension and, perhaps eventually to a shift, of strategic systems away from populations. Perhaps only through development of capabilities to continue his inevitable conflicts in space, can man justify any hope of realizing his ancient dream of peace on earth.

V

AMERICA IN THE SPACE AGE

*Whether they will or no, Americans must begin to
look outward.*
ALFRED THAYER MAHAN

The most sacred of American traditions will face their harshest challenges in the complexities of our technological future, and in the endless depths of space. In the coming decades, strategic weaponry of such mighty destructiveness will proliferate among the world's leading nations that any large-scale conflict on earth would strike a catastrophic, perhaps mortal, blow to civilization. This poses the question whether deployment of strategic weapon systems should be confined to our planet, in view of our consistent and apparently continuing failure to control armaments or avoid war by agreement. It appears likely that weapon stockpiles and expected levels of violence on earth, resulting from future wars, could eventually be reduced if strategic capabilities are extended into the space arena. Military motivations for such an extension exist naturally. In a time of onrushing technology and its determined use by the Soviet Union to gain new strategic advantages against earthbound bombers, ballistic missiles and submarines, there are growing military reasons why the United States as a deterrent power should begin to work seriously toward the strategic survivability which can be achieved by systems in deep space.

Consideration of this potential has been inhibited in the United States by fears of a new escalation of the arms race which might result from so-called de-stabilizing capabilities, and by diversion of funds from space activities as a result of the war in Vietnam and domestic urban problems. Apparently as a result of these fears and distractions, Presidents Eisenhower, Kennedy and Johnson took steps which led to the Space Treaty, a document which has further dampened consideration of strategic space systems, at least by the United States.

One result has been that the only two U.S. programs for the development of manned military spacecraft, Dyna-

Soar and MOL, each have struggled for six years after inception without ever receiving adequate funds to proceed to flight testing. Dyna-Soar died a lingering death in 1963, and MOL in 1969. Even NASA, having developed through the Apollo program the necessary basic vehicles and equipment for deep-space flight and lunar exploration, has for years been denied support for any coordinated plan to utilize and extend those capabilities beyond the first few flights. The areospace industry, which is a primary resource of United States brainpower and advanced technology, and which has been developed and organized at great cost and effort, is faced with funding cutbacks, employment reductions, and an increasingly less certain future.

MILITARY ASTRONAUTICS AND POWER CONCENTRATION

Inhibition of the development of the military potential of space in the United States is enhanced and compounded by a more fundamental factor, which is the traditional American distrust of bureaucratic concentrations of power. While the magnitude and costs of the task of developing strategic space systems appear comparable to familiar large efforts such as strategic bomber and missile developments and the Apollo program, space has no limits and the operation and technological updating of such systems would continue indefinitely into the future. And near-orbit systems are only a beginning. Strategic space capability can be truly effective only if far-orbit and interplanetary space is opened up.

Because of the technical scope and difficulty of the task, the essentially infinite size of the arena, and the fact that it is not an enterprise having any defined end, the exploration and use of space, particularly in the military sense, may, aside from the process of government itself, be the greatest impetus to bureaucracy in all history.* The task cannot be matched in this respect by past examples of exploration and military action. The objects of earthbound exploration have been the oceans and continents, which are limited in extent, in a way that space is not. Moreover, past exploration, occupation and development of new territories, have not required the difficult technologies and intricate specialization of individual effort whch are inherent features of astronautic activity. History's military conflicts may have involved more total mobilization of resources, but only for temporary periods, not much exceeding five years for either of the two World Wars.

This is a challenge to a deeply rooted aspect of the American character and the traditions of the Republic. Particularly distrusted are concentrations of power in the military, especially when no immediate necessity exists such as the threat of shooting war. Wariness of the professional military is typical in the United States, traditionally a land of the citizen soldier. This fear has almost certainly been a central factor in United States hesitance on the issue of the military in space since the first days

*By bureaucracy is meant a large, more or less formal, rigid administrative hierarchy, ordered along lines of authoritarian discipline controlled from a central seat of power. For present purposes, this definition includes officialism in all spheres of human activity, including the military, corporate and labor as well as government. This definition specifically does not emphasize the connotation of inefficiency, lack of imagination and red tape. While such connotation often applies within the ranks, the fact is that bureaucracy can be and has been used effectively by talented leaders, in the service of many imaginative and constructive, as well as more sinister undertakings.

of the space era. By that time the American ballistic missile effort had resulted in both Army and Air Force military-technical organizations which had adequate launch vehicles, operational know-how, and technical talent to permit initiation of space exploration and use. The most efficient alternative, both technically and administratively, would have been to let one of those organizations proceed immediately with an integrated national space effort. President Eisenhower, however, not only because of his concern about arms escalation, but mindful also that twentieth-century conditions were already imposing upon the nation a heavily bureaucratic character, including a large permanent military establishment, apparently hesitated at the prospect of an expanding astronautic bureaucracy under military aegis, which might increase military influence to unprecedented proportions.

By fiscal 1958, the strategic missile program had swollen the Air Force budget to 19.7 billion dollars, or about 26 percent of the total federal budget, as compared to only 11.1 and 11.8 billion dollars for the Army and Navy respectively. Planning and design for the first U.S. manned space program were already underway in the form of the Man-in-Space Soonest (MISS) program within the Ballistic Missile Division of the Air Force. Instead of permitting the Air Force to extend itself into space, however, President Eisenhower initiated the National Aeronautics and Space Act of 1958, under which responsibility for the space program was divided between the civilian NASA and the Department of Defense. Under the provisions of this Act, the decision as to which is the responsible agency in any particular case rests with the President. This gives the President strong influence on the growth and activities of both organizations, allowing them to be balanced against one another to prevent either from

178

achieving preponderant influence, economically or within the scientific-technological-industrial communities with which they must work. The Army's space engineering capability was in effect immediately liquidated with the transfer to NASA of the Von Braun team. The Air Force's manned space project was also transferred to NASA where it was continued as the Mercury program. Later, in 1961, Air Force plans for a manned lunar expedition (LUNEX) were also transferred to NASA where they became a starting basis for formulation of the Apollo program.

This tight control over development of military space capability, and over growth of a potential Air Force astronautic bureaucracy, is evidenced by the fact that later in 1963, even when the Air Force MOL program was finally approved, its management structure was set up separately and was made directly responsible to the Department of Defense, rather than to the regular Air Force organization, as had been the case with ballistic missile programs and the previously canceled Dyna-Soar. By fiscal 1970, as a result of this clampdown, and a buildup of conventional forces and strategic missile submarines, the Army and Navy had been gradually restored to budgetary parity with the Air Force. In that year, the Army, Navy and Air Force budgets were 26.4, 24.4 and 26.2 billion dollars respectively.

Such controls and balances bring with them the inevitable price of red tape, duplicated effort, reduced efficiency and interdepartmental struggles. As a result, there is the critical risk that exploration and assessment of the military potential of space might be sufficiently impeded that a potential aggressor, not so shackled, could achieve a technological surprise. Yet such checks and balances are inherent in the tradition and pattern of American government, as necessary to the maintenance of po-

179

litical stability. President Eisenhower forcefully expressed his concern with this problem in his farewell address on January 17, 1961:

> This conjunction of an immense military establishment and a large arms industry is new in American experience. The total influence—economic, political, even spiritual—is felt in every city, every statehouse, every office of the Federal Government. We recognize the imperative need for this development. Yet we must not fail to comprehend its grave implications. Our toil, resources and livelihood are all involved; so is the very structure of our society.
>
> In the councils of government, we must guard against the acquisition of unwarranted influence, whether sought or unsought, by the military-industrial complex. The potential for the disastrous rise of misplaced power exists and will persist.
>
> We must never let the weight of this combination endanger our liberties or democratic processes. . . .
>
> The prospect of domination of the nation's scholars by federal employment, project allocations, and the power of money is ever present—and is gravely to be regarded.
>
> Yet, in holding scientific research and discovery in respect, as we should, we must also be alert to the equal and opposite danger that public policy could itself become the captive of a scientific-technological elite.

This much-discussed plea, from a President's last official counsel to the American people, expresses a central dilemma of modern democratic societies. It is a struggle with conscience, awareness of the challenges of the future, but frustration because meeting those challenges seems to require actions in ways somehow inconsistent with historical traditions and beliefs. There is apprehension about regimentation, the concentration of power in elites, and large permanent military establishments. Yet the present and future seem to demand these of any society which is to survive, compete and provide leadership in an advanced industrial and scientific age.

Regardless of the sincerity and determination of our efforts to avert it, the onset of officialism is as inevitable as the advance of technology itself. As technology frees men from the constraints of nature, it increases their dependence upon one another. It has the effect of posing large-scale problems which can be attacked only with large centralized organizations, which are in turn made more efficient by technological advances in the automation of administrative functions. Examples of massive twentieth-century tasks already imposed on the United States are shown below:

MASSIVE TWENTIETH-CENTURY AMERICAN EFFORTS

Task	Direct Cost (current dollars)
World War I	$ 32 billion
World War II	$ 313 billion
Manhattan Project	$ 2 billion
Korean War	$ 18 billion
Ballistic Missile Programs	$ 50 + billion(?)
Apollo Program	$ 25 + billion(?)
Vietnam War	$ 79 billion (est. through 1969)
Supersonic Transport	$ 5 billion (?)

Each of these tasks has produced and will continue to produce lasting changes in the American way of life. Government, the military, business and labor—all are taking on the characteristics of large, permanent and highly organized structures, where the importance of the common man seems to diminish, and that of the organization and its elite seems to grow.

VISION AND PRACTICALITY: AN AMERICAN DILEMMA

It is easy to understand why adaptation to these hard realities of organizationalism, though almost inevitable in as innovative and adaptive a society as the United States, would be a slow and painful experience. A century of the down-to-earth struggle of exploring and developing the continent induced a strong spirit of individualism, as well as thrift, conservatism and concentration on the immediate.

This heritage has contributed strongly to the survival and growth of America during its pioneering and industrializing phases, but tends to weaken public support of exploitation in new technological areas requiring large-scale, costly efforts, which offer no promise of immediate payback, and which are not comprehensible to the general public. Not that America has lacked its Bushnells, Wrights, Mitchells and Goddards, but although these American visionaries produced the first submarine, the first airplane, the first significant demonstration of bombardment from aircraft, and the first liquid rocket, it was not America but the culture of Europe which had the initiative to mount the large efforts needed to reduce these concepts to practical usage. Recent examples are the German development of the ballistic missile in the form of the V-2 rocket and, on the basis of that V-2 technology, the Soviet initiation of space exploration with the Sputnik and Vostok satellites. Von Braun and his European team have provided much of the impetus and critical talent for the American space program. Anglo-French initiative in the Concorde project has impelled the world toward supersonic transport aircraft. Edward Teller, a European, was largely responsible for promoting the American H-bomb project. The atomic bomb might appear to be an exception until it is realized that the initiative and talent were supplied by refugee Europeans such as Albert Einstein and Enrico Fermi, and the money was risked by the United States only under pressure and secrecy of wartime conditions, and by the decision of an elite with no reference to the public at all. Under different circumstances, had not providence taken responsibility for this decison from the people and placed it in the hands of an enlightened elite, a Stalin, Hitler or Mao might have been first with nuclear weapons, a sobering thought indeed.

The characteristic American skepticism toward visionary thought and hesitance in its pursuit, and the disturbing implications for the future if these attitudes are not overcome, have been expressed forcefully by Professor Charles H. Townes, Nobel physicist and a principal pioneer of laser technology in *Science,* February 16, 1968:

> My belief is that knowledgeable and responsible people, in trying to judge carefully and not run too much risk of being wrong, have almost inevitably been too shortsighted. Furthermore, planners, in trying to be realistic and faced with tough budgetary decisions, all too frequently find themselves convinced only about what can be demonstrated, and hence their programs are unhappily limited. Science fiction and human need seem to have frequently been more reliable guides to predicting long-range technological developments than sober scientific statesmen.

183

... I am genuinely concerned about what seems to me a trend in the United States toward emphasis on the shorter-range goals and overconcentration of attention on utility to an extent which may well limit our technological productivity and leadership in the future. . . . It is clear that among the many fields where we face decision now are high-energy physics and space exploration. Both are exciting, but expensive. Very little utility can really be predicted for high-energy physics and little for much of space exploration. Yet we must examine them from both cultural and utilitarian points of view, and with such things on our conscience as the myopic tendencies of the past. And if in these fields or others we are found shortsighted, too lacking in daring, or too indifferent to forward-looking dreams, the pace of science and the impact of technology are now sufficient that our limitations will be obvious not only in the nation's future and the eventual judgment of history, but also to us personally, and in our lifetime.

Although Townes is presumably speaking in the context of nonmilitary technology, his basic meaning is clear, and relevant to the present discussion. It is simply that if the United States is to maintain leadership in the development and application of advanced technology (and certainly military space capability is a case in point), then traditional American attitudes must be broadened to include the audacity to make commitments and take risks against futures sufficiently distant that they do not permit the comfort and security of our yet being able to define them in all their details.

Lest the preceding comments appear to be an unreasonably hard indictment of American attitudes and capabilities with regard to new technological enterprises, it must be recognized that the picture is far from uniformly discouraging. There are at least two bright factors which are so apparent and important that ignoring them would be a serious omission.

First, American initiative and leadership is unquestioned and unchallenged in the area of electronics and computer development and application, the importance of which in shaping the future can hardly be grasped, let alone overestimated. The reason for this American ascendance may lie in a basic characteristic of electronic technology. Its progress does not depend on coordinated development and operation of gigantic vehicles, vast test and launch complexes and far-flung tracking and communications networks such as those associated with aerospace systems, which are not profit-oriented and which require large bureaucratic structures for centralized management of the many government, military, industrial and university organizations necessarily involved. Rather, electronic and computer progress seems to spring mainly from numerous, more or less spontaneous and usually profit-oriented inventions and developments, involving relatively small devices and components. Such developments can occur in modest laboratories of individual research centers and companies, and although sprouting somewhat independently, they seem through the dynamics of information-flow in the technical community and the marketplace, to combine quickly and naturally, producing a proliferation of increasingly advanced capabilities. It is hard to imagine how any process could be better matched to the traditional American economic system, and the phenomenal rate of such developments must be expected to continue, enhancing progress in aerospace systems as well as countless other areas.

Second, it must be noted that although European initiative was critical in imparting early momentum to

185

such new fields as submarine warfare, air power, commercial jet and supersonic aircraft, ballistic missiles and astronautics, the United States has, in time, become clearly predominant in all of these areas, with the important exception of military astronautics.

Here, however, the critical phrase is "in time," and the critical danger is that determined Soviet efforts in forging ahead in military astronautics could lead to some kind of technological surprise. It is stressed that this is exactly what almost happened in the case of ballistic missiles, where the United States overtook and surpassed the Soviets only by a crash military-industry program requiring more than a decade and costing tens of billions of dollars. In such a situation involving military space developments, there would be no assurance that sufficient time would again be available for a late-starting crash effort to be effective.

A UNITED STATES SPACE FORCE?

The dark fact cannot be avoided and it is no accident, that initiative and leadership in missile and space development has come not from America, but from the original experimenters in twentieth-century bureaucratic organization, Nazi Germany and Soviet Russia. The former sought to dominate the earth, and the latter seems intent on dominating not only the earth but space as well. The Soviet Union, with audacity and the efficient use of central planning and authority, has developed a first-rate national space effort which is evolving and growing in a determined manner. The Soviets make no managerial distinction between their miltary and nonmilitary space activities, and while they have until recently played down the military implications of their work, even this thin mask seemed to be disappearing with the unprecedented statement in November, 1967, by Col. Gen. Tolubko, then First Deputy Commander-in-Chief of the Soviet Rocket Forces, that all Soviet satellites and space vehicles including Sputnik 1, had been launched by Soviet rocket troops. He went even further in intensifying the astronautic image of the Soviet military:

> The old image of the earliest defenders of Communist gains was a man with a rifle, or a Red Guard on a horse-drawn machine-gun mount.
> A man near a missile pointed into cosmic space— this is the image of the modern serviceman, who not only mounts guard over the security of our Fatherland, but also participates actively in scientific research and in the conquest of near and outer space.

The United States space programs have been able to do little more than match Soviet progress at probably far greater cost, and show scant evidence of coordinated direction even for the near-term future. Air Force plans for more ambitious programs have been curtailed and, as the Apollo program achieves its culmination of manned lunar landings, the NASA budget shrinks with little clear prospects for further manned space exploration.

If this lack of planning, direction and support for American space efforts is not to result in irreparable yielding of leadership to the Soviets, a national commitment must be made soon to a permanent and ongoing program for the exploration and use of space, for military as well as nonmilitary purposes. Whether such a commitment should be in the form of an integrated program, with no distinction between military and nonmilitary activities as in the Soviet Union, or divided as in the United States, is a secondary question.

Arguments that the United States could not sustain the economic burden of an expanded space program, divided or integrated, would appear to be based more on subjective opinion than hard evidence. For while it is true that national defense budgets have increased considerably in dollar amounts over recent years, the phenomenal expansion of the American economy as a whole has actually resulted in a continuing decrease in defense expenditures as a percentage of the Gross National Product! During World War II, national defense budgets peaked at about forty percent of the GNP, and in fiscal 1952, during the Korean War, defense expenditures reached eighteen percent of the GNP. As the American economy has expanded, defense costs have shrunk in their relative economic importance. In fiscal 1958, at the height of the strategic bomber buildup and the early surge of the ballistic missile programs, the Department of Defense budget amounted to less than ten percent of the GNP, and by 1970 they will have declined to less than nine percent despite the costs of the war in Vietnam. The Air Force budgetary predominance, which apparently concerned President Eisenhower and probably Presidents Kennedy and Johnson as well, has been gradually eliminated since the creation of NASA, and the individual service budgets hold steady at about three percent of the GNP in each case.

This suggests that, as the Apollo program draws to an end and expenditures on it tail-off, a further initial national space commitment of at least five billion dollars or so a year could be undertaken with little if any dislocation of the national economy. If Vietnam expenditures decrease, this commitment could be expanded to much greater proportions even if total space and defense expenditures continue to dwindle as a percentage of the GNP. Even if Vietnam expenditures were not to decrease for a long time, the total national space effort could, if necessary, be expanded to a truly large scale with far less economic impact than the defense costs of, say the Korean War.

The concept which naturally suggests itself is the eventual creation and growth of a fourth major service, a United States Space Force, which might function at budgetary parity with the Army, Navy and Air Force. If such a service existed, say, in 1975, when the GNP is conservatively projected at over one trillion dollars, and even if the individual service budgets had each continued its longer-term decline to as little as two percent of the GNP, then the Space Force funding would nonetheless amount, on an equal basis to about twenty billion dollars annually. This would be far more than adequate to support development and initial operation of the key building blocks for strategic space capability described in Chapter III. Thus, not only would commitment to such a program appear economically feasible for the United States, but the military portion of it might be incorporated into a new major service, the economic influence of which could eventually be raised into mutual balance with the other three.

THE CHALLENGE OF THE FUTURE

As population continues to grow, and technology advances, the functions and problems of society become more complex. The processes of production and distribution, the provision of a proliferating variety of services, the maintenance of national security, the opening up of new opportunities in the oceans and in space and, especially, the job itself of governing all these activities, are so complex and interrelated that the means by which they were managed in the past are inadequate to the

189

future. It is increasingly evident that the only way to cope with these gigantic tasks is by the use of new information-handling techniques based on high-speed computers, and streamlined planning and management procedures, and that these methods will inevitably lead toward larger and more centralized organizational forms.

The rate of corporate mergers continues to increase, and big business becomes the rule rather than the exception. Labor unions begin to resemble, in size and organizational character, their traditional adversaries the corporations. The government expands its scale of operations and influence, including the gradual collection of a vast file of personal information on each citizen and organization in the nation (and many outside the nation). And the military services, because of their special dependence on and utilization of technology, control ever greater destructive capabilities and exercise ever wider influence in the political, technical and educational communities within which they must work.

It is this potential impact of a miltary astronautic bureaucracy and not, as we have seen above, the economic one, which could be a primary reason for concern. It is an important matter, and one which warrants serious consideration as a political and sociological question. Yet an expanded military space effort, as important a factor as it may be, should not be the sole focus for these kinds of fears and apprehensions. It is but one major aspect of the more general drift toward organized officialism.

This apparently irreversible trend in human affairs gives rise to grave concerns about preserving the rights and privacy of individuals, and indeed what is really meant by individual privacy and rights. Yet reluctance in accepting the large, permanent organizational structures necessary for tasks requiring vision, long-term planning and consistent support could be a serious obstacle to the maintenance of general world leadership in the future. This is certainly true in regard to space, and seems to apply in other critical areas as well—such as the solution of urban problems, where the regional and hierarchial fractionalization of governments and jursdictions is increasingly evident as a basic impediment to effective civil systems planning and management.

As the present and future bring on bureaucratic structures of increasing scope, both military and non-military, it becomes clear that the creation and management of such structures within a democratic society is perhaps one of the most fundamental challenges this nation could ever face.

Whether such demands and stresses of onrushing science and technology can be accommodated within the traditional framework of the American Republic, or whether the inevitable stretching and remolding of institutions may result in an essentially modified kind of society, and what that society may be like, are questions of surpassing significance for the United States and the world.

BIBLIOGRAPHY

Arendt, Hannah: *The Origins of Totalitarianism*. New York: Meridian Books, Inc., 1958.

Beaton, Leonard and John Maddox: *The Spread of Nuclear Weapons*. London: Chatto and Windus, for the Institute of Strategic Studies, 1962.

Bloomfield, Lincoln P. (ed.): *Outer Space—Prospects for Man and Society*. Englewood Cliffs, N.J.: Prentice-Hall, for the American Assembly, Columbia University, 1962.

Brodie, Bernard, *Strategy in the Missile Age*. Princeton: Princeton University Press, 1959.

Clarke, A. C.: *The Promise of Space*. New York: Harper & Row, 1968.

Clausewitz, Karl von: *On War*. Washington, D.C.: Combat Forces Press, 1953.

Cook, F. J.: *The Warfare State*. New York: The Macmillan Company, 1962.

Cooperman, David and E. V. Walter: *Power and Civilization—Political Thought in the Twentieth Century*. New York: Thomas Y. Crowell Company, 1962.

Frutkin, A. W.: *International Cooperation in Space*. Englewood Cliffs, N. J.: Prentice-Hall, 1965.

Galbraith, J. K.: *The New Industrial State*. New York: The Macmillan Company, 1968.

192

Gibney, F. B., and G. J. Feldman: *The Reluctant Space-farers*. New York: American Library, 1965.

Glasstone, Samuel (ed.): *The Effects of Nuclear Weapons*. Washington, D.C.: U.S. Government Printing Office, rev. ed., 1963.

Goldsen, Joseph M., *International Political Implications of Activities in Outer Space: Report of a Conference*. Santa Monica: The Rand Corporation, Report R-362-RC, May 5, 1960.

———, *Outer Space and the International Scene*. Santa Monica: The Rand Corporation, Report P-1688, 1959.

Golovine, M. N.: *Conflict in Space—A Pattern of War in a New Dimension*. New York: St. Martin's Press, 1962.

Goodwin, Harold L., *Space: Frontier Unlimited*. Princeton: D. van Nostrand Co., Inc., 1962.

Horelick, Arnold L., *Outer Space and Earthbound Politics* in *World Politics*, vol. XIII, January 1961, p. 323.

Jessup, Phillip C. and Howard J. Taubenfeld, *Controls for Outer Space and the Antarctic Analogy*. New York: Columbia University Press, 1959.

Kahn, Herman: *On Thermonuclear War*. Princeton, N. J.: Princeton University Press, 1960.

———, *Thinking about the Unthinkable*. New York: Horizon Press, 1962.

———, and Anthony J. Wiener, *The Year 2000*. New York: The Macmillan Company, 1967.

Kennon, E. A. and E. H. Harvey: *Mission to the Moon*. William Morrow & Co., 1969.

Knorr, Klaus: *The International Implications of Outer Space Activities*, in Goldsen (ed.): *Outer Space in World Politics*. New York: Praeger, 1963.

———, *On the International Implications of Outer Space* in *World Politics*, vol. XII, July 1960, p. 564.

Lapp, R. E.: *The Weapons Culture*. New York: Norton, 1968.

Liddell Hart, B. H.: *Strategy*. New York: Frederick A. Praeger, Inc., 1957.

Nieburg, H. L.: *In the Name of Science*. Chicago: Quadrangle Books, Inc., 1967.

Rabinowitch, E., (ed.) : *Man on the Moon—The Impact on Science, Technology and International Cooperation*. Basic Books, Inc., 1969.

Raymond, Jack: *Power at the Pentagon*. New York: Harper & Row, 1964.

Rechtschaffen, O. H., Lt. Col. (ed.): *Reflections on Space —Its Implications for Domestic and International Affairs*. Colorado: U. S. Air Force Academy, 1964.

Richardson, Lewis F., *Statistics of Deadly Quarrels*. Pittsburgh: Boxwood Press, 1966.

Schelling, T. C.: *The Strategy of Conflict*. Cambridge: Harvard University Press, 1960.

———, *The Military Uses of Outer Space: Bombardment Satellites*, in Goldsen (ed.): *Outer Space in World Politics*. New York: Praeger, 1963.

Schlafly, Phyllis and Chester Ward: *Strike from Space*. New York: Devin-Adair Company, Inc., 1965.

Sheldon C. S., 2nd: *Review of the Soviet Space Program* (with comparative U.S. data). New York: McGraw Hill, 1968.

Sokolovskii, V. D., Marshall (ed.): *Soviet Military Strategy*. Englewood Cliffs, N. J.: Prentice-Hall, Inc., 1963.

Stillson, Albert C.: *The Military Control of Outer Space*. New York: Journal of International Affairs, vol. 13, no. 1, 1959.

Wilson, Glen P. (ed.): *Soviet Space Programs: Organization, Plans, Goals and International Implications*, Staff Report Prepared for the Use of the Committee on Aeronautical and Space Sciences, United States Senate. Washington, D.C.: U.S. Government Printing Office, 1962.

INDEX